With Life and Laughter

D1073359

With Life and Laughter

The Life of
Father Miguel Agustin Pro

Gerald F. Muller, CSC

BOOKS & MEDIA

BOSTON

Nihil Obstat:
John P. Lynch, CSC,
Censor Deputatus

Imprimatur:
†Leo A. Pursley, D.D.
Bishop of Fort Wayne-South Bend

Library of Congress Cataloging in Publication Data

Muller, Gerald F. (Gerald Francis), 1927-
    With life and laughter : the life of Father Miguel Agustin Pro / Gerald
F. Muller.
        p.   cm.
    Previously published: Notre Dame : Dujarie Press, 1969.
    ISBN 0-8198-8281-X (pbk.)
    1. Pro Juárez, Miguel Agustin, 1891-1927. I. Title.
BX4705.P72M8   1996
272' .9'092—dc20
[B]   96-2915
                                                        CIP

    Acknowledgements: The author wishes to thank the following for their
generous contribution of time, talent and charity to make this project
possible: Mr. and Mrs. Emilio Rivero del Val, Brother James Weston CSC,
Brother Myron Bachenheimer CSC, Raymundo Bonilla, and Gary Werther.

    In keeping with the decrees of the Roman pontiffs and in particular
those of Pope Urban VIII concerning the beatification of the blesseds and
the canonization of the saints, I do not give to facts and expressions,
particularly such expressions as "saint, sanctity, miracles, etc.," any other
sense than that authorized by the Church to whose judgment I humbly
submit.—The Author

Designed by: Helen Rita Lane, FSP

Originally published by the Dujarie Press
Copyright © 1969, Dujarie Press

Copyright © 1996, Daughters of St. Paul

Printed and published in the U.S.A. by Pauline Books & Media, 50
St. Paul's Avenue, Boston, MA 02130.

Pauline Books & Media is the publishing house of the Daughters of
St. Paul, an international congregation of women religious serving the
Church with the communications media.

1 2 3 4   99 98 97 96

Table of Contents

Chapter One

One misty, chilly November morning in 1927, a slender, young priest was led before a firing squad in Mexico City and was shot. The man was Miguel Agustin Pro, S.J., and today he is world-famous because of his life of charity, suffering and practical jokes. Father Pro had committed no crime. As a member of the Society of Jesus, he had worked hard and patiently to bring bread to the poor and the Eucharist to the faithful. Like all priests, he was hated and hunted by the secret police of the capital and by the army throughout the Republic of Mexico. For this reason, after he was finally captured, he was killed without a trial. That was many years ago, but he is not dead. He is with Christ the King for whom he lived and died. If the miracles and favors which are attributed to his intercession are any indication of his present condition, then he must still be very, very busy. More than five thousand of these have been reported and the number continues to increase daily. His tomb in the Jesuit crypt in Dolores Cemetery attracts a constant stream of visitors who pass through the blue doors of the entrance. Above it can be seen his bas-relief portrait etched in concrete. They descend the narrow, steep staircase to place their hands on the gray granite slab behind which his remains rest. They leave long-stemmed gladioli and red carnations, light fat yellow candles as mementos of their visit and ask him for help in their needs. An ancient religious, Brother Luis Sanchez, S.J., greets the pilgrims, answers their questions and gives them pictures of the martyr and slender booklets that describe his life. Their pilgrimage ended, they climb the stairs and linger near the green wrought-iron fence encircling the crypt at ground level. This is weighed down by stone slabs that tell of the endless favors wrought through his intercession. When she was still alive, the martyr's sister, Ana Maria, often came to visit the tomb. Blessed with a marvelous memory and the tenacity to survive many sufferings, she remembered her late brother most vividly. This writer is deeply indebted to her for many of the incidents that will be described in the pages that follow.

Who was Miguel Agustin Pro? What did he do in life to make him beloved by so many such long years after his death? In all but a few respects, Miguel Agustin was quite an ordinary person. Too many biographers have stressed his love of fun, his humor, his capacity for practical jokes. Yet his sister, Ana Maria, who was younger than he and learned much about his youth from her mother, insisted that Miguel Agustin was a very serious person. The humor he displayed and the jokes he liked to play were purely spontaneous and only occasional. It is in his letters that his serious attitude and the quiet depths of his personality can be seen most vividly. It is interesting to note that not one photograph taken of him from his childhood until the day he fell before the firing squad can be found that shows him smiling.

Miguel Agustin Pro was born on January 13, 1891, in the village of Guadalupe, four miles southeast of Zacatecas in central Mexico. The third child of Miguel and Josefa Pro, he was taken three days after birth to the Franciscan monastery for baptism. Father Luis de las Piedras, a Franciscan priest who had recently returned from a pilgrimage to the holy places of Palestine, used water from the Jordan River for the ceremony that made little Miguel Agustin a member of the people of God. The same water which John the Baptist had once used for the baptism of Christ was used to make Miguel Agustin a member of the Mystical Body of Christ. It was a good beginning, and a harbinger of greater similarities between Leader and disciple that would culminate in a bloody, sacrificial death and the glory that follows such an offering.

The boy's father made a comfortable living for his wife and little daughters, Maria Concepción and Maria de la Luz, as a mining engineer in one of the richest silver mining areas of the country around Zacatecas. A tall, benevolent, dignified man, Señor Miguel Pro was a valuable worker for the government. Besides his work for the government's Agency of Mining, he owned two of his own mines. At times, private mining companies called on him for help. He had the rare skill of finding veins of mineral after they had been lost. Workers sometimes found themselves digging out worthless dirt instead of the soil glinting with gold or silver ore that could be refined into shining, precious metals. Because of his gift for finding lost mineral veins, Señor Pro also worked garnet mines and even owned one. He was at home in the shafts that went straight down in search of material as well as those which burrowed down into the earth, leveled off and then crawled back up to the surface. Knowledge of techniques to use in both types of mines was invaluable for him.

Miguel Agustin's mother, Josefa Juarez de Pro, was a small woman with profound understanding of her children and people. She had a great love for them which led her to give of herself for their comfort and welfare. From his earliest years, Miguel Agustin had a deep attachment to her, and one of her tears did more to correct his faults or punish an escapade of naughtiness than a scolding or a slap from his father.

Señora Pro was a gifted cook of fine pastries and special holiday dishes. She had the help of servants in the kitchen and house, which left her free to look after her growing family, her large comfortable home and endless charities for the poor. There were plenty of poor people in the mines, and Señora Pro went to their families with food, medicine and kind words. She did this long before federal agencies came to fill the yawning void left by too many who did not know or care about the needs of the poor.

From infancy, Miguel Agustin grew up a very happy child but he proved that he could be very serious, too. He had boundless energy and also traits of a bad character. At times he was impossible in his demands, and then his mother had to use all her wisdom, patience and tact to make him realize his mistakes, repent and begin correcting them. He always got along well with younger children, and his own home had plenty of playmates. Miguel Agustin Pro had no fewer than four brothers and six sisters. Besides Concepción, who was called Concha by her family, and Maria de la Luz, there were Josefina who died while still young, Ana Maria; Edmundo; the twins, Amelia and Amalia, who lived only a few days after birth; Alfredo, who died as a child; Humberto and Roberto. With so many brothers and sisters, Miguel Agustin was never without companionship, and most of his activities were enjoyed at home surrounded by his loved ones. Miguel Agustin was only a year old when his family moved to Mexico City. Here he learned to crawl, once terrifying his mother by inching his way along a ledge high above the street. Rescued from this adventure, he learned to hold himself erect and to take his first steps. Before long, he was saying his first halting words. After that he began experimenting with the song-like Spanish phrases he would learn to use with relish for the rest of his life.

At the age of four, Miguel Agustin was stricken with a severe and mysterious illness. He became listless and stooped.

His dark eyes, once snapping with enthusiasm or sparkling with joy, stared vacantly at nothing. For a whole month, his condition was unchanged. Doctors knew neither the cause of the illness nor its treatment or cure. The boy even forgot how to speak during this period. Other childhood diseases came to complicate matters. While his fever soared and physicians despaired of saving his life, his father had a sudden inspiration. He scooped up the tiny, fevered body of his boy into his arms and carried him to a picture of Our Lady of Guadalupe hanging on the wall.

"My mother," he cried in anguish, "give me back my son!"

A moment later, a great tremor passed through the child. The boy fell into a deep sleep after days and nights of exhausting pain. When he awoke, his recovery was certain. The doctors, who had predicted that the child would either die, or if he should survive, be mentally handicapped as a result of the illness and high fever, had to admit that the cure was miraculous. After a few days, Miguel was able to speak again.

"Mama," he told his astonished mother, "I want *cocol!*"

While she went happily to fetch the kind of bread he had liked so much before his sickness, she offered jubilant prayers of thanks to God and Our Lady of Guadalupe for her son's complete recovery. Years later when avoiding the secret police amid the religious persecution, Miguel Agustin Pro would sign his numerous letters and notes in the code name, *Cocol.* The young priest who risked his life to bring the bread of the Eucharist to hungering souls had not forgotten his cure in childhood, nor its source.

Before long the happy shouts of the restored Miguel Agustin were filling the patio and rooms of the Pro home in Mexico City. So great was his gift for acting and mimicry that one evening his father brought home a small theater complete with curtains, scenery and properties. All that the boy needed were the puppets for actors and his mother soon found these for him in the Alameda. This was the big central park of the city that is full of old shady trees, formal flower beds and vendors moving sedately under clouds of orange, yellow, red and blue balloons.

Monterey, just south of the Texas border, became Miguel Agustin's third home when he was about six years old. There, in a rented house not far from that of Governor Reyes, the boy watched the changing of the guard several times a day to the brassy music of a military band. Always fond of music and quite a gifted guitarist, Miguel Agustin watched the smartly uniformed, precision-marching soldiers come and go, and he dreamed of becoming one of them. Soon he was the proud owner of a military uniform and a bright flashing sword. His games were suddenly all war games and he delighted as most children do in playing "hurt" so that Concepción, now a Sister of Mercy, in his make-believe world could nurse him back to health on the "battlefield." There is a popular story, probably more legend than truth, that tells of Miguel Agustin's using his sword to whack off the heads of his sisters' dolls one bright morning while the girls were at Mass. Tears and wails of consternation filled the house after their return until Señora Pro promised to buy them new ones. Señor Pro took young Miguel Agustin aside to assure him that a man who makes a woman cry is a coward. Sticky glue failed to put the heads back together or attach them to the ragged bodies of the dolls, and the small soldier spent the fiesta without his usual supply of candy or coins. What is most certainly true is that the Pro children were taught from early years to respect, love and obey their parents. It is not surprising that this trait was later to be one of Miguel Agustin's strongest as a Jesuit priest even when he was doing his most dangerous apostolic work in the persecution. At times his superiors would tell him to go into hiding because his life was in danger and the noose was tightening around him. He would obey at once, spending long days, some-times weeks, in a stuffy room, while outside, the scarcity of priests and the needs of so many people filled him with longing to help them. But obedience was what was asked at the moment, and for him that was God's will.

Monterey celebrated its religious festivals with great joy, splendor and song. Miguel Agustin liked that. During the Corpus Christi procession, he delighted in carrying a long, lighted candle almost as tall as he was along the route ahead of the priest who brought the jewel-encrusted monstrance in which the Blessed Sacrament rested.

"Mama," he said with a great sigh of joy after returning home, "I want to go to a procession that never ends!"

Strangely enough, when the parish priest asked Señora Pro to send her boy over to the church to become a server, Miguel Agustin would not hear of such a thing. It hardly mattered anyway, because soon the Pros were busy boxing their belongings and preparing for another move, this time to Concepción del Oro, not far from Saltillo.

In their new parish, Miguel Agustin received his First Communion from the hands of Father Correa who in 1927, only a short time before Miguel Agustin, would give his life also as a martyr for the Church because of the hatred of the implacable and godless government leaders.

Schools were poorly organized in the little town, and Señor Pro spent as much of his leisure time as possible educating his children. Miguel Agustin was not a brilliant student. Nor did he spend much time with his books. His memory was remarkable, but his accomplishments in scholarly pursuits amounted to learning to read and write and work simple arithmetic problems. His father was able to spend less and less time going over his lessons with him. Once Señor Pro was called back to Monterey by company officials to investigate a gold mine someone was trying to sell to their company. Señor Pro went up into the mountains to find a cave where the rock glittered with gold-like particles. He scratched the rock with a knife and collected the sparkling fragments in a paper bag. While doing so, he noticed that no gold appeared deeper in the rock. He knew that gold ore never looks like gold but is found in black rock. Closer observation proved that all the particles were similar in shape and size. He discovered that the supposed mine was a fraud. It was an old trick to shoot against the rock walls with a shotgun using cartridges filled with real gold fragments instead of lead pellets to deceive buyers. With his usual honesty, Señor Pro told the company officials that the mineral they thought was gold was nothing of the sort. The mine was a fraud, and the swindlers had promised a great sum of money if he would cooperate in selling the cave and surrounding land to the company. This he had refused to do because he would not compromise his high principles for any amount of money. His task accomplished, he hurried back to his work and family in Concepción. There, he employed a private tutor for his children, since he found less and less time to instruct them.

When he could sneak away from his books and assignments, young, vigorous Miguel Agustin found much pleasure in hiking in the hills, climbing the rocky sides of mountains and following the bush-bordered streams as they meandered along. He liked to take his older sisters along with him so that they could "see more of the sky," as he liked to put it. He learned to ride horses and mules and more than once fell from his proud place in the saddle. He even had a penchant for falling off such vehicles as trains! Yet in spite of his misadventures, he was never seriously injured. But his carefree days of freedom were rapidly drawing to a close.

In 1901, he was ten years of age, and it was time for him to take up serious studies. He would no longer have a string of tutors with varying degrees of ability. Concepción was not the place for a young man to become learned. Señor Pro turned his attention to Mexico City and made arrangements for Miguel Agustin to be enrolled in the Colegio San José as a day student while living with relatives in the city.

When the train chugged into the dusty little station of Concepción, Miguel Agustin stood on the platform with tears in his eyes. He would miss the hills and streams and the rough miners to whom he had carried water and candy as they waited in line for their pay. But most of all, he would miss his family from whom he had never before been separated. With much kissing and sobbing, the goodbyes were murmured. His boxes were piled aboard the sooty train and white handkerchiefs fluttered in farewell. Then he was gone. How surprised the heartbroken boy would have been could he have foreseen how brief would be his sojourn in the capital.

Chapter Two

Only a few months after his arrival in Mexico City and his enrollment in the school of San José, Miguel Agustin Pro became seriously ill. His uncle with whom he lived summoned skilled doctors, but they were neither able to diagnose nor effectively treat the illness. The boy's stomach was painfully upset, but how to deal with the problem? Uncle Florentino sat down to compose a gently phrased letter urging Señor and Señora Pro to come to the city to see their son and at the same time visit relatives. The Pros came at once and were alarmed at Miguel Agustin's loss of weight and energy. After a brief visit, they hurried him home with them to Concepción del Oro, and there he gradually regained his health.

The following year the problem of finding a suitable school again arose, and this time Maria Concepción's boy-friend suggested the Colegio Acuña in Saltillo. Since he was a teacher, a close friend of the family and almost engaged to Concepción at the time, they heeded his advice. Señor Pro made arrangements to enroll Miguel Agustin in the school as a boarder. Saltillo, after all, was much closer to the mining town of Concepción del Oro than was Mexico City. The school was shining new and the faculty was said to be excellent. Only one thing had been overlooked while investigating its glowing educational possibilities for the boy. No one pointed out to the devout Catholic Pros that the Colegio Acuña was a Protestant establishment.

From the very beginning, Miguel Agustin was not happy in his new scholastic surroundings. When he arrived in the dining room for his first meal with the other boarders, he was greeted by a loud shout of welcome. He had hoped to take his place among them quietly and unobtrusively, but now he was unnerved and miserable as he hurried to his place embarrassed and self-conscious. The company and the food did little to settle his uneasiness, and on his first night in the boarding school, he cried himself to sleep.

Things did not improve with time. A photograph of the boy snapped in the garden of the school shows more clearly than words his loneliness and longing for home. He is seated on the broad, flat edge of a fountain. Dressed in a dark sailor-like suit with short trousers, he swings his thin legs nonchalantly and holds a wide-brimmed felt hat in his hands. But his face is sad and his large dark eyes are haunted by sorrow as they look beseechingly into the camera.

On the first Sunday of his stay at the school, he was alarmed because none of the boys seemed to be readying themselves for Mass. After waiting for some time, he hurried to the school's director and asked, "May I please have permission to attend Mass at a nearby church?"

"No, Miguel Agustin," the man said quietly. "There is no need for that. You will be able to attend chapel services right here at school later this morning."

"But I'm a Catholic; I am obliged to attend Mass on Sunday."

"Unfortunately, Miguel Agustin," the director explained patiently, "this is not a Catholic school. Since our rules state that boarding students must attend chapel services here, you will have to abide by them."

Trapped and despondent, Miguel Agustin had to obey, but he was soon at his desk scratching away at a letter to his father informing him that he had been enrolled in an institution that did not tolerate religious liberty. He begged his father to come and take him home at once. The only way to have the letter mailed was to send it through the director's office where it was read, censored and in some manner rerouted—probably to the nearest wastebasket. In any case, the letter and those that followed which told of the boy's religious imprisonment never reached Señor Pro. Week followed week, and each Sunday Miguel Agustin found himself unable to assist at Mass.

During his stay at the school, he became a good friend of the cook. One day he sauntered into the kitchen to ask, "May I help you in any way?"

"Surely," the woman said, "but let me finish this work before I give you a job to do."

"I'll help you right now," Miguel Agustin volunteered.

The cook was busily stuffing meat balls into a tube of bread like dough. Miguel Agustin watched her for some moments and then came over to assist her in his own way. While the meat balls fell with perfect regularity through the dough tube, Miguel Agustin, instead of holding the bottom of the tube to catch and hold them there, popped one after another of them into his mouth. So quickly and cleverly did he do this that the cook was not even aware of his actions until it was too late.

"Miguel Agustin, what have you been doing?" she asked angrily after she dropped the last meat ball into the dough and found to her surprise that none of those which had preceded it had been held in place inside the tube.

"Having a little snack," said the boy.

"But that meat wasn't thoroughly cooked!" she explained. "You are going to be very sick! It will serve you right, too!"

The cook had uttered a prophecy. Before long, Miguel Agustin was writhing with the pain of a stomachache and a doctor had to be summoned to his bedside.

"You had better inform the boy's parents," the physician told the alarmed director. "This boy is very ill!"

The circumstances left the school's leader no other choice. Although he had kept the news of Miguel Agustin's inability to attend Mass on Sundays from Señor Pro, he was not able to withhold information about his health—especially since it was now so precarious. As soon as the letter arrived in Concepción, Señor Pro set out at once for Saltillo. He gathered his son's belongings and hurried the sick boy home to recuperate. Only after his return to his family did Miguel Agustin reveal that he had not been enrolled in a Catholic school at all. Horrified by the narration of his experiences, his father never sent him back.

From then until he reached maturity, Miguel Agustin was educated at home by private tutors. Erratic at best, his schooling came to an end when he was about fifteen. Later, having decided to study for the priesthood, he would have to spend years making up for his lack of classical training. Knowing little Latin and even less Greek as a result of his desultory training, he would have to start at the beginning in classes of bright-eyed youths, years younger than he was.

During his years of adolescence, Miguel Agustin Pro often went down into the mines. There in the long, dark, humid galleries the stooped miners clawed at the ore with their picks and shovels, prying out riches in which they had little share. And often above-ground, Miguel Agustin carried a heavy basket filled with food, clothing and medicine as he walked the dusty roads beside his mother on her missions of mercy to the poor families of the miners. She wished him to see firsthand the plight of the poor and to appreciate their problems and need of help. The sensitive young man never forgot the lessons he learned during these visits. Although the miners worked long hours far below the sunlit surface of the ground, they were never able to earn enough money to provide more than the stark necessities of life for their loved ones. Having no share in the ownership or operation of the mines, they toiled endlessly and hopelessly like drones. Accidents and cave-ins were commonplace. The serious injuries that frequently resulted from these required medical attention and months of convalescence. But doctors were few and hospital accommodations for these poor people were practically nonexistent. To dull some of their pain and frustration, the rough miners frequently squandered their small earnings on liquor and drank away their troubles for a few hours, only to find worse problems facing them in the sober gray dawns that followed.

Faced with such appalling conditions, Miguel Agustin's mother resolved to open a hospital for the miners. General apathy from the neighbors greeted her enthusiastic appeal for assistance, and she finally went ahead with the work almost by herself. A house was found, leased and divided into wards. Three doctors agreed to donate their services to the poor. Pharmacists sent boxes of free medicines. The task of managing and finding helpers for the daily work of the hospital was left to Señora Pro, her older daughters and Miguel Agustin. It was sometimes his task to move the heavy patients from one bed to another or from bed to wheelchair and back. In the humble hospital established by his mother, he learned many things about charity for those in need.

Good and necessary as the work for the sick and the poor was, Señora Pro's hospital of San José benefited only a portion of those in need in the little community. The project lasted a year and a half before a new mayor came with some of the revolutionary ideas that would soon tear all Mexico apart in one of the most terrible social revolutions in history. By decree of the mayor, the hospital of San José was forbidden to take in only the poor and abandoned. Deluded by his false concept of freedom, he insisted that all classes of people be admitted to the small wards regardless of creed, economic condition or social position. To make matters worse, he forbade any priest to bring the last sacraments to the dying in the little hospital. With the quick flourish of his pen as he placed his signature on the document, the new mayor put an end to Señora Pro's dream. She wanted to help heal the broken bodies of the poor miners or to prepare their souls for approaching death by making available to them the Last Rites of the Church when they were most in need. Señor Pro ordered his wife and family out of the hospital. The Señora was pained at seeing the destruction of this work of charity and the death of her young son Alfredo added to this suffering. Her last baby, Roberto, had only recently been born, and it was Miguel Agustin's pleasure and privilege to act as godfather for the wailing infant. Later he would look after his godson with special solicitude and love, even sharing a cold prison cell with him during the last few days of his life on earth.

The miners were discontent at their miserable condition. Open threats to take matters into their own hands if the absentee owners of the mines did not heed their demands for better wages and safer working conditions made life difficult and dangerous for Señor Pro. He stood as a government agent between the frustrated, overworked laborers and the heedless owners who were far away from the problems in place and perception. Señor Pro finally resigned as adviser of the company of mines. Unable to find employment in a larger city in which Miguel Agustin could go on to higher education, he applied himself to his work and office in Concepción del Oro. He had so many new duties that he decided to make Miguel Agustin one of his assistants.

At the age of fifteen, Miguel Agustin began his work as a clerk in his father's office. He helped with the mail, studied the many case histories of mines involved in lawsuits and filed documents away in the archives. One asset which the young man possessed to a remarkable degree was his memory. He could remember minute, complex details of a case history as well as the place in the files in which he had buried the documents relating to it. Even after Señor Pro had moved his wife and family to Saltillo where the younger children could be better educated, he kept Miguel Agustin with him during the week to work in the office, allowing him to visit the family on weekends. Here, surrounded by his brothers and sisters, he played his guitar and led the singing of ballads and folk songs. Never tiring of music, he often jumped to his feet, pulled Concepción from her chair and to the plink of guitars and the crackle of castanets performed the joyful, whirling native dances of his country.

Miguel Agustin was very fond of girls but he never had a sweetheart. Three sisters who were friends of Concepción were also his friends: Angelita, Emilia and Eva Cepeda. A lively exchange of letters went on between Miguel Agustin and these three girls during his weekly absences and some of them have been preserved. For example:

"To Angelita: Man possesses the secret of greatness in his intelligence; woman in her heart. The heart is great when it loves nobly. Long live women!" He signed this note "Homobono"—a good man.

In a note to Emilia he became even more eloquent. He wrote: "The influence of women upon civilization and the greatness of nations is so efficacious and mysterious that the social condition of its first rank can be deduced with certainty by the social condition of its second. Long live women!" After an excellent meal prepared by this young woman, Miguel Agustin sent the following thank you note: "I never imagined you could make *palotes* with such perfection and if it weren't that I am overjoyed at having this beautiful postcard, I can assure you I would send you much more praise...."

For Eva, he once composed this lyrical verse:

> When shadow enwraps the objects
> And the night grows quiet,
> In its black carriage, softly
> Over the earth it passes...
> When the moon with its silvered rays
> Spills upon the fields,
> And the mirror of the limpid lake
> Reflects its pallid light
> When the burning breath of the sun
> Follows the cold of the frozen night
> And the birds shiver in their nests
> Upon the weak branch
> And when in the distance
> Is heard the roar of the restless sea...
> Finally, when the mysterious night
> Rules sad and quiet...
> That which every being ought to do then
> Is...to go to bed.

Miguel Agustin did not always place the correct letter in the proper envelope. Once, while distracted in his father's office, he happened to slip one of these nonsense-notes into the envelope addressed to a priest while sending the priest's letter to the girl. When the cleric called this to his attention, Miguel apologized and tried to explain his mistake. Later, he did exactly the same thing by mistake, but with more serious consequences.

His mother received the letter he had written to his Protestant girl friend, and the girl received his mother's message. Miguel Agustin was going through a period of crisis and doubts about his faith at the time. He was brusque and uncommunicative—something unusual for the vigorous, energetic, affable young man. He had long been in the habit of going to Mass frequently, going to confession and Communion at least once a week and of saying the rosary each afternoon with his family. Suddenly, he gave the impression that religion meant little to him, and he did not attend Mass as frequently as before.

Señora Pro was deeply disturbed by her son's change of attitude, but she believed that it would disappear after a time, so she quietly waited and prayed. During a chance visit to the house of the parish priest, Miguel Agustin was introduced to guests of the pastor, two Jesuit priests. These clerics were the first Jesuits with whom he was to have close contact. During their conversation together, one of them suggested casually, "We are on our way to the hacienda of San Tiburcio to give a mission. Don't you want to come with us?"

Something stirred deep within Miguel Agustin and he felt a great urge to accompany them. "I'll have to ask permission," he said.

"We'll wait for your return," said the priest, smiling.

Miguel Agustin hurried home to ask his delighted mother for permission to go with the priests. It was granted at once, and he was soon on his way with the two Jesuits. During the days of the mission, he wrote two letters that he placed in the wrong envelopes. Eva, his Protestant friend, received the message meant for his mother, and Señora Pro received Eva's note. The results were a disaster in one way and a blessing in another. Properly incensed by what she had read in her letter, Eva promptly returned to his house all of the young man's small gifts to her. And the Señora later had the joy of knowing that Miguel Agustin had not only made the exercises of the mission but had gone to confession, received holy Communion and had regained his peace of soul. He had also acquired a deep respect, admiration and love for the Jesuit Order as he saw its ideal and work personified in his two new friends. Later, as his vocation to the priesthood became clearer in his mind, he would have no trouble deciding which religious community to join.

Miguel Agustin returned from the hacienda in his usual good spirits. Later after visiting the tomb of Friar Juan Crisóstomo Gomez, granduncle of Señora Pro and her saintly confessor, he exclaimed, "I want to be this kind of saint: a saint who eats, sleeps, plays practical jokes and works many miracles!" His idea of the spiritual life and the pursuit of perfection was quite different from that of the old, dead priest who left his crucifix and instruments of penance, the discipline and hairshirt, behind in Señora Pro's keeping. In his own way, Miguel Agustin was to achieve his desire and destiny. He was to live a deep spiritual life, but bubbling at the surface of his personality was always great joy, ready wit, spontaneous jokes and lighthearted laughter that made him so attractive to all he met.

Smoking was one of the earthly joys for which Miguel cultivated a taste, but he did not want his father to know that he was gradually developing the bad habit. So he smoked in secret and tried hard to rid himself of the telltale odor lingering on his breath and clinging to his clothes. One day he slipped out onto the balcony that encircled the patio of his home to see if it was safe to light a cigarette. He was surprised to see his father standing directly below him looking up curiously to watch his movements. Miguel Agustin happened to lean over the railing to hear what his father was saying when the cigarettes tumbled out of his shirt pocket and went spinning in crazy circles down on his father's head. Miguel's face flushed a deep crimson, and he hurried downstairs to explain.

"What are these things?" his father asked when the youth reached the patio, embarrassed and out of breath from his hasty descent. He held up the cigarettes that he had retrieved from the floor for him to see.

"Why, those are a new brand of very fine cigarettes I want you to have," Miguel Agustin told him, an air of innocence in his manner and tone of voice. That night at dinner,

Señor Pro ended the meal by pulling out the offensive cigarettes for a second time and offering one to his son at the table. Miguel Agustin politely refused it and decided that he had much office work to attend to at once. He excused himself and hurried from the room. But his habit had not been broken. Soon he had purchased more cigarettes for himself. He continued to enjoy smoking alone and as far from his father as possible. Later, of course, he smoked in his father's presence and Señor Pro raised no objections. When his son was a man, he was free to act accordingly.

Each year during the long school vacation, Miguel Agustin's family was reunited in Concepción del Oro. Their evenings together rang with the sound of music. Yet in spite of their joy at being together again, tension hovered over the house, the dusty town and the restless country. The momentum of the revolution was growing in a gradual but powerful crescendo, and its signs were as unmistakable as they were unpredictable. Several riots broke out in the mines near the town. Once in their fury, the miners came storming up to the Pro home demanding access to the archives and files so that they could destroy the deeds of the owners. Only the frantic prayers of the family members and the timely arrival of federal troops saved them all from serious harm.

The year 1910 brought important changes for the Pro family and their country. In August, Maria de la Luz entered the convent in Aguascalientes to become a nun. At the same time, the fires and forces of the revolution that would shatter Mexico began to erupt violently. For five years they would rage and change the entire pattern of life for Miguel Agustin and each member of his family.

Chapter Three

The entrance of Maria de la Luz into a convent came as a severe blow to Miguel Agustin. With her and Concha he had shared many happy experiences: working, vacationing, singing, dancing and talking of serious things. Without Maria de la Luz the family orchestra was depleted and the family fiestas were far less lively. After her departure, he lamented, "How beautiful heaven must be since one must pay for it so dearly!"

Miguel Agustin was now eighteen years old. His long years of work in his father's office had become a monotonous blur of routine clerical duties which no longer interested him. Dutiful son that he was, he hid his discontent from his parents. His services were needed, at least for the time being. He would continue the daily round of chores: opening and answering the mail, filing reports, and studying the case histories of so many mines. His constant interest in the work and life of the miners brightened his otherwise dreary days. He loved people and delighted in communicating with them in order to advise, cheer and help them. From time to time he sought advice and direction from Jesuit priests who taught in the school of San Juan Nepomuceno in Saltillo. During the coming months, he laid careful and quiet plans to join their community. Even his parents were not aware of his plans.

The entire Pro family traveled to Aguascalientes to witness the taking of the habit by Sister Maria de la Luz and the reception of First Communion by Humberto, her godchild. This double ceremony took place on February 2, 1911, and the whole family received Communion with the exception of Miguel Agustin, who refused. He was enduring a time of doubt about his faith with great uncertainty while a violent struggle raged in his soul. During Mass and at the breakfast that followed, he burst into tears, and he related later that "he felt as if the heavens had fallen upon his head." His mother watched him helplessly, her heart aching with sorrow, but she did not scold him. Instead, she prayed fervently to God for her son. While Concepción stayed with her sister at the convent for several days, she was strongly attracted to religious life. Soon after making her desire to become a nun known to the superior, she was received as a postulant into the same convent. It was some days later that the Pro family returned to Saltillo without the two older sisters. Their absence from home caused Señora Pro acute sadness and loneliness. Therefore, her husband decided that Miguel Agustin should stay with his mother in Saltillo to console her. In that city he went to visit Father Telésforo Corta, a Jesuit who, like all the Jesuits there, knew the Pro family quite well. This priest wisely and prudently studied Miguel Agustin's character, helped him resolve his doubts and guided him for four or five months. At last Miguel Agustin sent a letter to Father Ipina, provincial superior of the Jesuits in Mexico, asking for admission into the Order. Father Corta sent his own letter of introduction and recommendation for the young man. Since the Pro family was well known, the answer came back quickly, accepting Miguel Agustin into the Order. Father Ipina assured him that his vocation was certain but that it was necessary for him to ask and obtain his parents' permission before he could enter the community. Thus one year after Maria de la Luz's entrance into the convent and six months after the reception of the novice's habit by Concepción, Miguel Agustin decided to leave his family and become a novice in the Society of Jesus. His decision was to come as a severe blow to his parents.

Miguel Agustin did not know how to ask such a difficult favor of them, but God made it possible for him to break the news rather indirectly. While suffering from a severe fever, he was confined to bed, and his father and mother watched beside him day and night. In his delirium, he let his secret escape by speaking of his forthcoming entrance into the Society of Jesus.

In spite of their sorrow, his parents willingly granted him permission to leave home to follow his call. Desiring to present his son personally to the master of novices, Señor Pro made the long, four-day journey south of El Llano at Miguel Agustin's side. There, on a quiet ranch not far from Zamora, he remained while his son made a three-day retreat. On August 15, the new novice came to visit his father.

"Miguel, my son!" Señor Pro said when he caught sight of the smiling, slender youth now dressed in the black cassock. In a touching and beautiful gesture, Miguel Agustin came up to his weeping father, dropped to his knees before him, joined his hands and looked at the ground. Señor Pro placed his hands on his son's head and prayed silently that God would abundantly bless this treasure he was offering to him. A little later he bade Miguel Agustin goodbye, climbed aboard a train and began the tiring trip home. It was to be a long and lonely journey.

Three other novices, all younger than Miguel Agustin, had received their cassocks during the same ceremony with Brother Pro, as he would now be called. Unfortunately, they felt that sanctity was only a matter of long, sad faces, endless prayers and unrelenting abnegation. To make matters worse, they soon became homesick and shed frequent tears over the fact that they were far from home and relatives. The humid climate and hot winds blowing mosquitoes from the swamps did little to cheer them, and Miguel Agustin's high spirits did even less. When he could stand the atmosphere no longer, he went to the novice master's room and knocked loudly on his door.

"Father," he said after being invited to enter, "I want to return to Concepción del Oro."

"Why?" Father Santiago asked, his eyes opening wide in mock surprise.

"Because before I came here I liked the Jesuits very much, but now they all repel me—beginning with you!"

Instead of angrily ordering the impulsive novice to pack his bags and leave the house, the understanding priest threw back his head and laughed. He motioned Miguel Agustin to a chair, and after casual conversation he explained that Miguel's fellow novices were younger than he. They were not so mature and were still uninformed about the essence of religious life. "You are older," he said, "and you have a happy disposition. That is a great blessing and I want you to use it to cheer up your fellow religious."

After their candid interview, the novice master often sent Miguel Agustin out for hikes in the surrounding hills with the other novices. Picnics were arranged for them with hefty baskets filled with thick sandwiches and delicious fruits of the region. Brother Pro's smile returned; his high spirits were given full sway. At the same time he slowly learned the rules and spirit which Saint Ignatius of Loyola had bequeathed to his community. Each day consisted of prayer, work, classes, exercise and recreation.

Feast days were special events with solemn high Mass and outings in the country for the entire day. During one of these some large, tasty avocados were found in the bottom of the picnic basket. Brother Pro took a bite from the one he had selected and cried, "Heavens above! If I had known that you had such avocados here, I would have become a Jesuit a long time ago!" Father Santiago, resting his back against a tree trunk, laughed and realized that Miguel Agustin had long forgotten his desire to return home to Concepción de la Oro.

"Here is a guitar," the novice master said, lifting the light instrument and offering it to him. "Let us hear you sing some of those mining songs you know so well."

Miguel Agustin needed no further urging. He took the delicate instrument into his hands, squatted down in the midst of his friends and was soon strumming it happily as he accompanied himself in a song. One by one the other novices joined him, and the afternoon was not complete until each had performed some dance indigenous to the region from which he had come.

One day the novices were enjoying recreation on the patio of their house when Father Santiago strolled in with a distinguished guest robed in purple.

"My dear novices," he said, as they rose swiftly to their feet and a sudden hush fell over them, "I have the honor of presenting to you his excellency, Archbishop Oroxco from Guadalajara."

The novices bowed and spoke their greetings. That did not satisfy the prelate, however. He wished to meet each of them one at a time, so a line formed and they came slowly up to him to be introduced and to speak briefly with him. Finally, Miguel Agustin found himself approaching the archbishop while he heard Father Santiago saying, "This is a new novice—very spiritual! Let's see Brother Pro. Come here and tell the archbishop some jokes as you do so often."

Miguel Agustin grasped the outstretched hand of the prelate, bent to kiss his ring and then raised his head to carry out the assignment. As he did, he noticed that Father Santiago was eyeing him with a threatening look that said "Beware!" He was suddenly not in the mood to tell funny stories, even though the archbishop encouraged him to do so.

After painful moments of silence, the novice master said abruptly, "Very well. You still do not know how to obey. That's enough."

Submerged under a vast wave of embarrassment and confusion, Miguel Agustin simply could think of nothing to say for once in his life. He slunk back into the ranks of his friends wishing he could suddenly become invisible. But the humiliation was quickly forgotten and even before the archbishop had concluded his visit, the vivacious novice was chatting easily with his friends, his hands punctuating the air to emphasize his words, his dark eyes riveted on his listeners.

On another occasion he helped his fellow novices celebrate a holiday by joining them in a vigorous baseball game. When it was over and the tired teams were returning from the grass-covered field, he climbed catlike in one bound to the top of a creaky platform behind the catcher's box and improvised a sermon. The perspiring athletes forgot their weariness as they galloped over to the exalted pulpit to hear whatever nonsense Miguel Agustin might think of on the spur of the moment. Laughter rippled through the youths at his feet, and some were so overcome by their mirth, that they hunched over and galloped off to regain their composure. Seeing his audience slipping from his grasp, he jumped down from the perch and trotted after them calling, "Don't go away, brothers! The sermon isn't finished yet. The preacher is going to climb back up there again." As he spoke he motioned to the platform. At that moment, he caught sight of the black cassock of Father Santiago suddenly materializing in the midst of the novices in their bright play clothes.

"What's going on here?" the priest asked.

After an awkward pause and some nervous giggles, one of the boys explained that Brother Pro had just been preaching a fine sermon. The novice master smiled and said, "Fine! Fine! I am sorry I came late. No doubt the speaker will do me the favor of starting from the beginning and giving his talk all over again!"

Knowing that he had to obey, Miguel Agustin climbed back up on his perch and gave the sermon a second time. The repetition lacked much of the zest and brilliance of his first performance, but Father Santiago was quietly amused.

A bond of deep friendship grew between these two men. From the beginning, the novice master perceived the silent, serious depth of soul in his energetic novice. He was perfectly aware that Miguel Agustin hid this facet of his personality from his companions the way Thérèse of Lisieux had done. Both knew that the most spiritual thoughts, feelings and insights lost their fragrance when exposed to the air of casual conversation. He noted, for example, that Miguel Agustin never spoke about his spiritual life, himself, his family or his past when surrounded by his companions. Only rarely did he speak of his saintly mother or of his aspirations. When he did, it was only to one or another of his closest friends and in private.

From the very beginning of his two-year period of training in the novitiate of El Llano, Miguel Agustin was aware of the kind consideration his director gave him. Who else was permitted to organize such frequent hikes, picnics and excursions? Who else could play the little practical jokes to cheer up the dour-faced novices and go unpunished and uncorrected? "If God, my Father had not given me such a novice master," Miguel Agustin later admitted, "I certainly would not have persevered in my vocation."

Not all of the novices who entered the Society of Jesus with him did persevere. This is not surprising since one purpose of any novitiate is to test one's vocation to determine if such a life is right for the individual. Yet Miguel Agustin never forgot vocations. His kind heart remembered them in thoughts, good wishes and prayers. He always remained their friend. This quality can be seen well in a letter he wrote to Father Santiago on April 5, 1925, from Enghien, Belgium, shortly before his ordination to the priesthood.

My very dear Father Master in Christ:

Among the first ones to whom I ought to announce the immense good fortune that God has given me is you, to whom by more than one claim I am indebted. On the 31st of August, I shall say my first Mass. What I feel, what I think, what is happening to me, Father, you will understand better than I am able to put into words. Ever since you gave me this blessed cassock, even to this day, special graces and favors have not been interrupted for me. A love truly of predilection that in all my religious life has been shown to me cannot be explained except by Jeremiah: "With age-old love I have loved you; so I have kept my mercy toward you."

You who knew me and who knows how in spite of my repugnance I was brought to the Society of Jesus can see how in me is fulfilled the letter of the law of the Psalm: "From the dunghill he lifts up the poor to seat them with princes, with the princes of his own people" (Psalm 113:7).

How did I come to this state? What are my claims? What are my merits? Only the mercy and love of God can explain them. How much, Father Master, I would like to speak to you for half an hour!

With what pleasure I would tell you so many things that cannot be said in a letter, but since now I cannot do so, I shall limit myself to ask your prayers to give thanks to God and to prepare me better for the reception of so great and divine a sacrament.

Of the four novices who began on the 15th of August in 1911, one has gone to heaven, the outstanding Brother Rodarte; another, Brother Campos, is in his second year of theological studies; the third...God knows where he is. And I, the last of the four who later made the vows of devotion, am going to be ordained.

Perhaps you will try to contact our poor little brother...[who left the community]. If you can, I beg you, Father, if it is convenient for you, give him this news and tell him that in my first Mass I will have him very much in mind.

Last year I left Sarria [Spain] where there were those with whom I lived in El Llano. Frequently, as Father Leobardo will have told you, we spoke of you with great consolation.

You cannot know, Father, how much good your words have done me, which you spoke one day before we left [the novitiate]. I came to your room and Brothers Pacheco, Campos, Amoz, Martinez and Quevedo were already there. You told me to come in and blessing me said to me, "This is also one of ours."

On more than one sad occasion, I have remembered those words and they have encouraged me very much because they were the judgment of my Father Master.

Bless your novice, Father Master,
who loves you very much in the heart of Christ.

With his superiors, Miguel Agustin Pro was always serious and sensible. With his companions, he was witty and full of mischief. Having completed a year of his novitiate training, he was one of those who welcomed the new group of novices to the sprawling ranch at El Llano. One of them later wrote: "Brother Pro came to my attention as soon as I arrived at El Llano. I saw him leaving the chapel with moderate pace, his eyes lowered and his naturally long face in repose but very pale. No doubt he was the victim, like many others, of the fever that was very common in that humid climate.

"He always seemed to me very humble and very friendly. Thanks to his spontaneity and happiness, he could talk of religious topics better than anyone else.

"In a notebook he had collected different prayers and thoughts of solid piety, proof of his good ascetical taste. On one occasion, he let me copy the things I liked most. It was good to read that handwriting of his, so clear and elegant. The principal point of his notes concerned the Sacred Heart of Jesus for which he had a solid and sincere devotion.

"What I admired most about him was his spirit of sacrifice and his ability to forget illness and the tribulations brought about by the social and religious miseries of the country. He knew how to keep everyone happy when he himself felt unhappy." He was to keep this quality all of his short life. He perfected it to such a degree that even when suffering terrible physical pain, he could keep it so well concealed under a serene exterior that an occasional constriction of his face was all that betrayed him. It was momentary, and only his keenest observers ever noticed it.

Brother Pulido was a friend of Brother Pro who came to El Llano as a novice in 1912. According to his contemporaries, Brother Pulido was "good as an angel and shy as a nun." He was also to be one of Miguel Agustin's first biographers. This guileless dove had scarcely come to roost in the novitiate before tricks were being played on him by the devilish and imaginative Pro. "His jokes were never vulgar," Brother Pulido admitted, nor was Miguel Agustin ever unkind in winning his laughs. A perfect mimic, Brother Pro could imitate his new friend's habits of speech and movement to the tiniest detail. Yet it was the sensitive new novice who noted the two facets in Pro's personality. "During the annual retreat," he observed, "the comic and talkative Pro changed into a Carthusian who spent more time in the chapel than anyone else. He was very careful to perform his acts of piety with scrupulous care."

However, such attention to spiritual affairs had not hindered him from finding a new hiding place every day from his fellow novice, Brother Francisco Altamirano, who was in charge of herding the others into second Mass each day. From childhood Miguel Agustin delighted in hiding things from those who were looking for them. When the opportunity now presented itself, he was most agile in finding hard-to-find places in which to duck, so that his friend would have to come looking for him after depositing the others in prayerful positions before the altar. As Francisco's footsteps approached and the scent of the chased became stronger, Miguel Agustin would jump out to startle the solemn prefect. Each day he found a different hiding place; each day there was a new surprise.

Later, after Brother Altamirano's transfer to the College of Saint Stanislaus some distance away, Miguel Agustin wrote to him as follows:

My dear Brother in Christ:

Surely it will be a surprise to you that I should be writing you. This probably would not have happened if I didn't understand your natural curiosity, which makes you want to know what happened here on the feast of the Sacred Heart. Holy Mass was celebrated for the community by Father Master with the usual solemnity for this great occasion. The chapel was beautifully decorated. The choir did not sing very well but the music wasn't too bad after all. Brother Cosio, the organist, played brilliantly even though he has studied music only one year.

At 5:25 in the afternoon, I carried my humanity on short steps up into the bell tower and clanged the bell heartily. The community came like a rocket to church, where Father Habig, in a trembling voice, recited the Act of Consecration. Father Master was garbed in the brand new cope. Father Macias with the cross and

Brothers Campos, Valdes, Amozurrutia and Carriedo
with the candles led the procession. Little girls dressed
like angels followed them, as well as three others
dressed as faith, hope and charity (a little bit sun-
burned). A small, elderly cowboy, with a blanket on his
shoulder and tottering on weak legs, carried the banner
of the Sacred Heart. Men followed. Then came a
woman carrying the banner of Our Lady of Guadalupe,
followed by many others....

Two years of training passed by in the novitiate of El
Llano. The days were full of quiet, prayerful reflection. There
were also unimportant incidents of mirth to enliven the rather
dull routine of daily duties and gradual growth. Miguel
Agustin was to be remembered for only two things: profound
piety and contagious joy. Nothing about him gave the slightest
hint of his future fame and nothing hindered his official acceptance into the Society of Jesus. On August 15, 1913, he made
his religious vows of poverty, chastity and obedience. The vow
formula, written in his own elegant handwriting, can still be
found in the archives of the Jesuit province of Mexico. To it he
later added: "I am glad I have made the vows. With my whole
heart I ratify my perpetual consecration to God." Having put
his hand to the plow, he did not look back. Grateful for the rich
graces God had given him, he looked forward to a new phase
of his religious life: long years of intellectual labor to prepare
himself for his goal, the priesthood and an active search for
souls.

Chapter Four

A month after his religious profession, Miguel Agustin Pro quietly began his study of Latin and Greek in El Llano. Life in the house of studies went on as usual, disturbed only occasionally by wild rumors of revolution in distant parts of Mexico. Miguel looked up from his book at the silver-green eucalyptus trees. They were reflected in the still water of the canal, which ran into the distance between green, flowering meadows. Miguel Agustin mused about his family so far away to the north. He rarely received news of them. Mercifully most of the details of social conditions around them at that time were hidden from him, because his superiors did not wish to reveal them. A serene atmosphere and peace of mind are essential for young students pursuing their education. Jesuit leaders, aware of Mexico's political and social unrest, resolved to keep their novitiate and house of studies at peace until forced to close it.

In the areas beyond El Llano the frightful fires of total revolution and civil war had exploded over a bewildered and frightened people. Religion, law and common decency were swept aside in the robbing and raping, burning and butchery that followed armies of generals and bandits across the land. In the west, General Obregón led his soldiers to victory and plunder. The bandit and cattle rustler, Pancho Villa, swept through and ruined the center of Mexico. In the east, Pablo Gonzalez led the attack on farms, villages and cities. Venustiano Carranza was the mastermind of this frightful civil war. He hoped, he said, to return the country to "constitutional normalcy" after General Victoriano Huerta had claimed presidential powers following the assassination of President Francisco I. Carranza had a peculiar way of restoring normalcy. The revolution he set in motion was soon raging beyond his control. Churches were looted and burned; clergy and religious were tortured and exiled or murdered. The rich were stripped of their property, and anyone who had worked for the federal government found himself out of work and in danger.

One of these was Señor Miguel Pro, who had worked long and hard as an Agent of Mines for the federal government. During almost the entire year of 1912 he remained at work as usual at his office in Concepción. He was astonished by what the revolutionaries and a mob of mining workers had done. All of the government buildings had been looted and burned during his absence. The Agency of Mines was now a gray mound of ashes with all the archives and furniture, his belongings, titles and degrees destroyed. Everything was gone. Even worse, some of his friends warned him that the mob promised to shoot him on sight if they ever saw him again. Because of this state of chaos and danger, he took the next train back to Saltillo. Federal troops still held that city, even though they were engaged in frequent skirmishes with the raiding parties of Francisco "Pancho" Villa.

Soon the news arrived that a main attack on Saltillo was imminent. That meant looting, raping, killing and burning as the revolutionary hordes were doing elsewhere. In those circumstances, the Pro family decided that Señor Pro should go to the capital to inform his superiors of the ruin of the Agency of Mines. Now, however, only a few trains were left in operation, and these were used for carrying troops. Since there was no means available to move the whole family at the moment, Señora Pro displayed the wisdom and courage she had always shown during difficult circumstances. Knowing that her daughter was in great peril, she asked her husband to take Ana Maria with him. She would remain at home with her three young sons, facing the danger with great faith and trust in God and in the Blessed Virgin. Señor Pro agreed. Leaving his wife, Edmundo, Humberto and Roberto behind, he set off on the long journey with Ana Maria. They took the last train for the south. It was a military train on which the Pros were the only civilian passengers. "You cannot imagine," Ana Maria recalled later, "what the landscape was like. All the railroad stations were burned. The huts, houses and cottages everywhere were lying in ashes. Then there was the nightmare of seeing the telegraph poles with corpses dangling from them. My heart was full of sorrow when I remembered my mother and brothers alone and surrounded by crowds fighting savagely."

When Saltillo surrendered a few days later, one of the first acts of the victorious Villa was to summon the Jesuits from their school of San Juan Nepomuceno and demand no less than one million pesos as tribute to the revolutionaries. Merchants and the landowners were also to be taxed. It was impossible to raise or find so large an amount of money. Therefore, priests and people were tortured, jailed and sent off into exile in the United States under the glazed eyes of drunken guards.

Life in the capital was dangerous and precarious at best for Miguel Agustin's father and sister. Señor Pro could find no one in charge at the government mining headquarters. His superiors had been substituted by personnel of the new regime. He and Ana Maria stayed at his brother's home for some time while looking for work. No work was available. Advised by a relative that he might find employment in Guadalajara City, he decided to go there and look for a residence for himself and his daughter. Railroad tracks had been blown up, telegraph lines severed and even mail service disrupted by the chaotic fighting. There was simply no way to communicate with other members of his family to the north or with Miguel Agustin to the south. Yet through traveling acquaintances or the providential passage of a letter, Señor Pro was able to contact his wife in Saltillo, telling her to bring the boys south to Guadalajara. She came shortly afterward to find Ana Maria in the home of an aunt and her husband absent, because he had returned to the capital seeking work. "What happened to my father," Ana Maria explained with the calmness and patience acquired over long years of privation and suffering, "happened to everybody." She continues: "The leaders quarreled among themselves. One would be shot and another would take his place. Every time a group of soldiers swept through a city, they would change everything. Each new band threw out the previous group. There would be a fight, and the others would move on. Finally, there was nothing to eat anymore."

Señora Pro's life in Guadalajara was "filled with a variety of tasks" so as to provide food and education for her children. "My mother was an expert in the art of fine cooking," Ana Maria has said. "She taught classes in fancy cooking to the women of society in a friend's house. She had to suffer terribly during this time, but always very patiently. If she is not in heaven, then no one is. Doctor Julio Franco, a close friend of our family, looked after us. The priest who conducted the school in which Humberto and Roberto had been enrolled also helped us very much. Both of these men knew how hard a time my mother was having and they were always willing to help."

The rumors that had rumbled like distant thunder in El Llano during the fall and winter of 1913 became awesome realities for Miguel Agustin Pro. On a sunny spring day he sat on the lawn with his friends to hear a talk by Father Benitez. Having fled from Durange with little more than his life, this Jesuit told of the conquest of the city by the troops of Carranza. Churches had been looted, the Blessed Sacrament profaned and statues smashed. Nuns had been raped, and the entire community of Jesuits had been forced to flee for their lives. Father Benitez predicted that what had happened in Durage would soon happen in El Ilano and its environs. The speaker left his young listeners to think about the atrocities he had described and their own precarious future.

Bit by bit, Miguel Agustin was able to piece together, in a terrible mosaic of confusion and disorder, the flight and misfortune of his family. It was hard for him to concentrate as he reviewed for final examinations. Now he knew that those he loved were living in hiding and in danger and that the hungry fires of the revolution were slipping closer and closer to his own house. Bandits did pretty much as they pleased in the streets of Zamora, and with the arrival of General Amaro leading some troops of Carranza, the city finally capitulated. From this base of operations, raiding parties were free to range at will into the surrounding countryside. Before long, they would be banging on the doors of the hacienda of El Llano.

Early August brought the opportunity for a great celebration in the Jesuit house. The rejoicing took place in spite of the revolution and the oppressive, mounting tension. One hundred years before, Pope Pius VII had lifted the ban of suppression that had for so long put an end to the life and work of the Society of Jesus. Using his gift for excellent drawing and lettering, Miguel Agustin busied himself producing large pictures portraying the history of the Jesuit Order with appropriate inscriptions for each. Dangling from a high stepladder and helped by his friends, he succeeded in hanging the pictures from the pillars to suspend them from the walls below the balcony. The holiday began with a solemn high Mass of thanksgiving and a procession honoring the Sacred Heart which wound through the rambling corridors of the big house. A program for the community followed, complete with declamations, poems and songs. In the evening, the young faces of those preparing for uncertain futures glowed in the light of Chinese lanterns dangling overhead.

And on a night shortly afterward, there were fireworks of a different kind. A band of twenty-two heavily armed soldiers of Carranza arrived at the hacienda, demanding entrance to the property. At one o'clock in the morning, they amused themselves by shooting in all directions and breaking into the ranch house not far away from the novitiate. They broke the furniture, cut the telephone wires and burned the account books. Satisfied with their vandalism, they galloped off shouting and shooting into the darkness. Awakened by the shots, Miguel Agustin's superiors rushed down to the church where they stood guard before the doors. When they heard the noises of the marauders growing fainter in the night, they returned to their rooms. On the following morning, Miguel Agustin found a bullet lodged in a wall of the sacristy where he worked. One of the priests found a similar wedge gouged out in the wall of his room. It was now evident that the community would have to be dispersed and preparations would have to begin at once. Delay was dangerous. Library books had to be packed into heavy boxes; the sacred vessels were buried under the floor of a rickety shop. Fine oil paintings came down from the walls and were sent off to the homes of friends for safekeeping. Secular clothing of many hues and colors arrived in appropriate sizes for each member of the community. It was time to think of disguises for the long, lonely journey into hiding and later into exile. Miguel Agustin acquired the tight-fitting clothes and wide-brimmed hat of a rancher. Dressed in this outfit, he entered the community room to bid goodbye to his friends on the afternoon of August 15, 1914. He made a last visit to chapel, where an empty tabernacle now greeted him. About 4 o'clock, with Brothers Campos, Caver and Rios, he left El Llano for the last time. On foot, they made their way to Zamora where dangerous days awaited them. In the home of Brother Rios' parents, they found a refuge and for several days had the immense consolation of being able to attend Mass and receive Holy Communion in the hospital chapel of San Bernardo. General Amaro soon put a stop to that by ordering all churches closed on the twentieth. All priests were rounded up to be imprisoned, tortured or forced to work as street sweepers.

For five days, the seminarians were unable to find a Mass being celebrated anywhere. Even worse, they were discovered in spite of their disguises. One day in front of the Hotel Mexico, officers of General Amaro shouted, "Look at those priests!" Seeing little point in hesitating to explain that they were not priests, Miguel and his companions took off at top speed with the soldiers in hot pursuit. Two devout old ladies helped in their narrow escape by opening their house and hiding the youths until the soldiers had dashed on past their door.

When the street was cleared of the military men searching for them, the seminarians stepped out cautiously only to be greeted by the high, sweet voices of children sitting on the curb: "Goodbye, Fathers! Goodbye." Under the circumstances, the young men decided it was better to ignore the shrill farewells. They ran back to the Rios home and comparative safety.

Having learned that two local priests lived in hiding on a hill near the town, Miguel Agustin and Brother Rios undertook the hazardous task of carrying food to them each day. Once, on their return from their errand of mercy, they saw a company of fifty revolutionaries riding toward them at full gallop. They plunged from the dusty road, and dashed into a field of tall corn. The sharp blade-like leaves slashed at their faces and hands, and they threw themselves on the ground. The kettle-drum roar of the pounding horse hooves increased and then gradually faded into silence. For more than an hour, the two young men remained in their hiding place. As they came out of their green blind, they stumbled upon a kind Indian who took them to his hut and gave them a meal.

On August 28, the Jesuit superiors made contact with their scattered members in Zamora and ordered them to proceed to Guadalajara. Led by Miguel Agustin, still dressed as a country boy, his sombrero tipped down over his eyes, they slipped out of the city gates at night while the guards snored at their posts. In a field outside they assembled and sent word to El Llano that they were still alive and in need of help. Father Maina came to them with a large basket of food. He heard their confessions, gave them his blessing and sent them on their way.

Rain began to fall and by the time they reached Ixtlan, they were drenched. With the help of an old burro they continued their tiring journey. When rumors reached them that bandits were in the vicinity, they hid for the day. Once they arrived in a tiny village where a fiesta was in progress. Bright flags fluttered from the balconies; music and laughter filled the air. The villagers caught sight of the fugitives, unshaven for days, and covered with dried mud from their long march. The people ran off in terror shouting "There they come! There they come!" thinking the bandits had arrived to rob and shoot them.

Having reached Negrete at last, they boarded a train that would carry them to Guadalajara. En route, Miguel Agustin played a fine role as the humble servant of his companions. He shined their mud-spattered shoes, fetched their suitcases and waited on them with obsequious obedience. On September 2, they arrived at last in Guadalajara and had breakfast with Señora Dolores Puga. More than a month before, the city had fallen to Carranza. He had promptly expelled all priests and foreigners and made life almost unbearable for its citizens. In the home of Señora Puga, Señora Pro found her tired and travel-stained son. For a moment their sorrows were forgotten in the wild joy of reunion.

Later that morning, Miguel Agustin went to share the privations of a scantily furnished apartment and to visit his brothers and sister. All of them had grown and changed considerably during the three years since he had last seen them. The short weeks that followed were to be the last that Señora Pro would enjoy with her oldest son. As long as the persecution of the Church continued, both fully realized that exile was the only means by which Miguel Agustin could continue his studies for the priesthood. After ordination, still many years in the future, he would be able to return to Mexico to carry on his Christlike ministry. Yet even to gain re-entrance to the land of his birth would prove difficult and dangerous.

The fugitive seminarians arrived in Guadalajara alone or in small groups. Guided by a Jesuit priest, they tried to maintain some form of community life even though they stayed with relatives or friends in different parts of the city. Thanks to a sketchy diary kept by one of Miguel Agustin's companions, their chaotic life can be seen in occasional glimpses. Obregón, the conqueror of Guadalajara, had ordered all churches closed. Priests were forced to say Mass in private homes, and just finding these secret meeting places was a hazardous, time-consuming task for the seminarians. Even to enter such a dwelling, they had to know the appropriate password, which at times was the sign of the cross on forehead, lips and heart. But this had to be changed when soldiers discovered it, and dressed in ordinary clothes, occasionally sneaked in to spy.

On one occasion, Miguel Agustin and his companions decided to assist at a Mass celebrated in Saint Teresa's Church, even though such an act was forbidden by Obregón. Warned that if caught while the Eucharistic Celebration was going on they would each be fined five hundred pesos, they went bravely in and fortunately were not discovered. To celebrate their evasion of the soldiers, they had a reunion in a private home afterward. Miguel Agustin entertained with his mandolin and songs. To cheer up his friends, depressed and uncertain of their futures, he often dramatized little skits in which he played all the roles himself, using quick changes of costume found on the spur of the moment. A perfect mimic, he made his audience laugh by imitating the fiery military leaders who aroused the emotions of the people in order to make them accept the new revolutionary ideas. During their brief times together, the seminarians prayed, discussed their activities for the next day, sang songs and hymns and recalled old happy times in El Llano.

They had ample opportunities to practice works of mercy. Miguel Agustin found a poor old woman dying in a hovel. For hours he stayed at her side, reciting aloud acts of contrition and confidence in God for her during her long death agony. Shortly before she died, he held his profession crucifix against her lips to kiss. Resigned to God's will and at peace, knowing she would not be abandoned in her last moment, she quietly breathed her last.

Sunday Masses were always interesting for Miguel Agustin. In the home of a companion, for example, he donned not only his cassock but also his black cape, which he daringly draped over his shoulders for this special event. The following week, he found himself in the home of a sympathetic Protestant, assisting at Mass in the midst of a large gathering of devout Catholics. Before long, their hiding place was discovered by revolutionaries who had grown suspicious at seeing the constant stream of people entering the house. At 10 o'clock in the morning, the revolutionaries who had surrounded the house were driven away in fright by a mob that swelled to marvelous proportions in a short time. They shouted, "Long live the Sacred Heart! Death to the constitutionalists!" The rebels who thirsted to bring the country back to "constitutional normalcy" were going to find it difficult to deprive ninety-five per cent of its citizens of the faith that had been rooted within them since birth and whose traditions stretched back four centuries. But they did their best. In Guadalajara, they used the old, lovely cathedral for their barracks. In order to save some of the sacred vessels, the books and the memoirs of Maximilian, the ill-fated former emperor of Mexico, Brother Juan Romero had to disguise himself before ambling in to look for the treasures. With his wide sombrero pulled down tightly on his head and a fat cigar smoldering in his mouth, he went about his chores. He was sick at what he saw. Broken bits of statues littered the floor. Altars had been profaned. Ornaments lay in rubble. Later, Brother Juan described for his companions the desolation as he pulled from his big sack each of the glinting gold chalices and dusty books he had been able to salvage and bring home in triumph.

By the end of September it was learned that the railroad line to Laredo, Texas, had been rebuilt after numerous bombings. The first day of October brought the scattered seminarians their orders to flee to the United States to continue their studies. They prepared for their journey into exile by attending Mass sung to the accompaniment of a piano. The consecration to the Sacred Heart was made in common and they hurried to the task of packing. Small groups of departing seminarians were formed, each leaving at a different time. Miguel Agustin was a member of the first group that boarded the train. He kissed his mother goodbye. The crushing pain in his heart at leaving her and his family surrounded by poverty and uncertainty was perfectly evident in his drawn face, but he did not cry. Neither did his mother who cheerfully and patiently bore this new cross as she had borne all those that had gone before it and that would follow. She watched his fluttering handkerchief waving goodbye to her until it blurred into the smoke and dust of the departing train. She would not live long enough to welcome him on his return to Mexico as a priest, but it did not matter. God's will be done. That was all that mattered, and it was enough.

Chapter Five

The battered train snaking its way north toward the United States puffed through miles of desert waste. Here and there derailed cars lay like dead animals on their sides, so broken and covered with rust that they were beyond repair. Many of the towns along the route were blackened piles of rubble and ruins left by bandits or rebels in their frightful passage. Ravaged by flames, fields lay mute and scarred, stretching way into the distance from both sides of the track. As the old train creaked closer and closer to the border, the number of ghost towns increased. The seminarians looked apprehensively into the distance where followers of Pancho Villa lurked, even though not actively engaged in bloody civil war. No one could be certain when they would spring again into their saddles and ride with guns raging and swords slashing to some new attack on the helpless.

With mixed feelings, the young Jesuits arrived in Texas, glad to have reached the safety of a free country at last after a long, exhausting journey, but sad at having been exiled from their homeland. In San Antonio, the Oblate Fathers gave them a warm welcome, but since the Mexicans spoke very little

English, they felt ill at ease in their difficult task of making themselves understood. Miguel Agustin Pro made a brave effort to speak the unfamiliar language, but he was not very successful. Fellow Jesuits met them at the train in El Paso, making them feel at home at once by greeting them in fluent Spanish. The exiles could not enjoy their company long, however. They were ordered by their superiors to proceed west at once to Los Gatos, California, a little south of San Francisco. Here they were to continue their studies and resume community life.

Another long and tedious train trip brought them to their home in exile—a wooden cottage at some distance from the big brick novitiate of the American Jesuit Fathers. The cold of November soon drove them into better quarters, this time on the third floor of the novitiate building where they studied and lived in cramped conditions. Father Piet, Brother Pro's new rector, now had two communities to care for, one American and one Mexican. He did much to make life for the exiles bearable despite lack of space and books. Language continued to be a nagging problem. When all else failed, including sign language, Miguel Agustin was forced to use Latin to express himself. No textbooks written in Spanish could be found so the teachers, Mexican exiles also, gathered the Spanish-speaking seminarians around a big table and taught them orally. The results were soon evident on examinations. The material simply was not being grasped. To make matters worse, an ancient oil stove coughed out more smoke than heat. Its fumes made eyes water and throats constrict into spasms of coughing. Education was not easy in the verdant, vine-covered hills of California.

During recreation, Miguel Agustin's high spirits helped his friends forget some of their troubles. He learned a few English words, most of which were slang expressions, and this merely whetted his appetite to learn more. Father Joseph F. Howard, S.J., one of his American fellow students in 1914, wrote:

Brother Pro was not long in endearing himself to us by his openness and general good humor. I can remember one small incident that took place not long after his arrival. We had the custom at Los Gatos of dividing into groups of three for evening recreation. This particular evening Brother Pro and I were in the same threesome. As I recall, Brother Pro's father was a mining man and Miguel was brought up in those surroundings. I believe, too, that this particular mine was an American operation, or at least there were Americans working there, and Miguel picked up something of their language.

In those early days of acquaintance, much of our conversation consisted in "How you say this?" or in Latin, "Quomodo dicis?" or "What does this mean...?" So in the course of our walk around the grounds, Brother Pro asked, "What does 'go to hell' mean?" In Latin we tried to explain "Ite ad infernum." He received the answer with amusement. But it was always my suspicion that he knew perfectly well what the expression meant all the time.

I would say that of all the Mexican Juniors who were with us for that short year, Brother Pro was the best liked and the one thought to be most like us [Americans]. He was always cheerful and friendly to all. He showed himself, even then, to be an excellent mimic, a gift he was not too free to use, especially if he thought his portrayal might hurt someone.

For all his humor and practical jokes, Miguel Agustin had the delicate sensitivity and charity to know how to control his gift of amusing others. He refused to hurt his friends' feelings in eliciting laughter.

Father Howard explains, "In learning English, in which, if I recall rightly, he never became proficient, he had a specialty. He did learn all the slang Americans would teach him. I should add that, due to the general idea in those days of what a saint should be, if we Americans were asked to vote on which of the Mexican brothers would someday be considered for beatification, I believe Brother Pro's name would be way down on the list. Yet, even then, he showed many of the characteristics that made him loved by the Mexican people and hated by the police."

Fortunately, that false idea of sanctity, symbolized by a pale, sad face and downcast eyes, endless prayers and painful flagellations, has been laid to rest. Pope John XXIII saw to that, and he based his convictions and behavior on the life of the Man in Galilee who lived a most ordinary life and saved the world by following his Father's will in obedience, love and joy.

It was difficult for Miguel Agustin to express his gratitude to the California Jesuits for their hospitality in welcoming him and his young companions into their midst. In a poem dedicated "To the Brothers of the Province of California," he concluded with these lines:

> Now at last the safest refuge is found for the tired sailors
> And a pleasant home is found for our labors; Here at last pain and sorrow are ended. You all will be to us as brothers related by blood, The help of the wretched, a kind and pleasant solace to us.

For one of his favorite feasts, Our Lady of Guadalupe on December 12th he wrote the following:

> To whom shall we hasten in search of consolation, without country, without family, without roof and without home?
> Only to you who left your throne there in heaven. In order to conquer the country [Mexico] you love to inhabit so well.
> O my Mother, you keep watch for us, wandering and exiled,

To return to our country which is the country
of your love;

You care for us who spend this hour at your side;

You care for us who place a flower at your feet.

What does it matter that death takes away our
existence

Suffering the bitter solitude of our exile,

If in the midst of our pains we feel your presence,

If we feel your mantle that covers us with kindness?

When final examinations brought a difficult school year
to an end, the Mexican exiles were ordered to Spain where
they could continue their studies in a Jesuit house at Granada.
Political and social conditions in Mexico were as bad as ever.
All hope of the fugitives' return to that country for an ordered
community life had been long since abandoned. On June 21,
1915, Miguel Agustin and his companions said goodbye to
their American friends in Los Gatos and boarded a train that
would take them east on the first leg of their long journey to
Spain. In El Paso, a stop of several hours allowed the weary
travelers time to visit friends, the Mexican Jesuits living in that
city. Too soon, they were once again aboard the swaying,
clacking train which carried them to New Orleans and a day of
sight-seeing in that humid, old hospitable metropolis. Having
finally arrived in Key West, Florida, they boarded a ship sailing for such divergent ports as Havana and New York City
before pointing its prow toward the rough, rumbling Atlantic
and the Spanish port of Cadiz. Not until late July did the
seminarians reach their new home in Granada in southern
Spain. Here Miguel Agustin was to spend five years pursuing
his studies of languages, rhetoric and philosophy. He also
learned as much as possible about the social conditions of his
special friends, the working class for whom he had long har-
bored a special attraction and a sincere love.

Chapter Six

Rising jewel-like on its three hills that overlook the fertile plateau around it, Granada traces its beginnings back to Roman times. It is world-famous for its beautiful Alhambra, the palace built by the Moors for their kings when they ruled Spain. In such historic and scenic surroundings, Brother Miguel Agustin Pro settled down to a life of serious study. Never a brilliant student, he pored over his books and managed to acquire average grades for his efforts. Having lost time for study in chaotic Mexico and in exile in California, he tried hard to regain his place in the humanities when other seminarians his age were studying theology. At the same time, he became one of the hardest working catechists in a dozen villages near the city. If Brother Pro left to others the honors of the classroom, he glowed with special brilliance during recreation, at concerts and in dramatic productions on feast days. Seminarians from many countries had come to Granada to study. One of these, Father Joseph A. Butt, S.J., an American, recalls several impromptu attempts by Miguel Agustin to cheer up his fellow students.

Books, studies and lectures were not the only things that occupied the minds and lives of the young scholars at Granada. Their spiritual exercises took up much of their time each day. Every seminarian also had an assignment or task to perform at certain times during the day so as to keep such a big house clean and in order.

Miguel Agustin's job was sometimes that of waiting on tables in the large echoing refectory. Beside the rector of the theological students, the Jesuit provincial of Spain and his entire council of advisors were seated at the head table. This group of serious, important men made their home in the same building and kept a watchful eye on the young seminarians around them.

Before each meal began, the food for the various tables in the dining room was placed, steaming and appetizing, on a big four-wheeled cart. Then it had to be pushed into the refectory after the saying of grace. Miguel Agustin always enjoyed doing this chore. "I don't want the rest of you straining your backs," he would say, bending over the cart with a pained expression on his face. He pretended it required all of his strength to push the vehicle forward. One of his fellow waiters would then rush to the door leading into the dining room. He would open it and stand at attention holding it while Miguel Agustin made his dramatic entrance. The other waiters trooped along like an honor guard in two files behind him, poker-faced and silent, while the voice of a reader droned like a lazy fly over the hushed room. The kitchen door opened out from one end of the long refectory while the head table with its many dignitaries stood at the opposite end, literally yards and yards away. Whatever happened near the kitchen door, therefore, could not be observed by the rector or provincial. Usually, if Miguel Agustin planned to give a short performance, he did it immediately after his entrance from the kitchen. As soon as the door swung open, therefore, all eyes of the waiting seminarians swung like beads of metal attracted by a strong magnet from their empty plates before them to the bent figure pushing the heavy cart. On one occasion while they watched in delight, the cart came lumbering through the door and stopped only a few feet inside the dining room. Something was wrong with one of the front wheels. Miguel Agustin, an expression of horror shrouding his face, trotted to the front of the vehicle to find one of its tires completely flat. The tire, of course, made of solid, hard rubber could not possibly become flat, but he pretended it was. He gave such a convincing performance that the seminarians at the tables began jamming napkins into their mouths to keep their laughter from exploding loudly and thus ending the show.

Miguel Agustin rushed to the back of the cart where he found an imaginary pump. In no time at all, he was back connecting the device to the valve of the front tire and pumping frantically with quick up-and-down movements, stopping only now and then to see that the tire was refilling properly.

The pantomime could last for no more than a minute or suspicion would be aroused in the mind of the rector who waited for the food cart to appear before the head table. Therefore, Miguel Agustin finished his act of pumping the tire very quickly, tossed his imaginary pump someplace onto the bottom rack of the cart and continued on his way between the tables with the serene and dignified air of a headwaiter.

Bringing the cart to a halt a short distance from the head table, he saluted the crucifix with a profound and reverent bow, then the provincial and at last his rector. This done, he lifted the different dishes from their places on the cart and carried them with a flourish to the waiting priests. The other waiters soon encircled the cart to do the same thing for their famished friends. Only the seminarians were aware of this incident, like many others, that occurred near the kitchen door. Fortunately for Miguel Agustin, none of them ever told the rector what they had witnessed. That would have put a quick end to the fun and merriment.

Before another meal, Miguel Agustin came rushing into the refectory wheeling his cart at top speed. He pretended he was driving a new, fast car. Cars had always fascinated him, and the faster they went, the better. But on this occasion as he made his way between the tables, something went radically wrong. The speed of the "auto" grew slower and slower until it came to a grinding stop. "Must be out of gas," Miguel whispered dolorously, opening the top of the "gas tank" and thrusting his finger down into it trying to feel if it had any "gasoline." Satisfied with his findings in the imaginary fuel tank, the young motorist decided to crank the "car." In those days, before automatic equipment that starts a motor in a moment, a clumsy iron crank was the common means of turning over the engine. Miguel Agustin was soon hunched over the front of the cart making wondrous faces as he tried with all his might to make the "car" start. There seemed to be no cough or response to his best efforts, so he moved the "choke" up and down. Nothing happened even after that encouragement. So he gave the cart a vicious kick that rattled the dishes on each of its trays and nearly spilled the steaming food.

One last try with the crank and the "car" began to purr, or at least Miguel Agustin pretended that it did and he took his place behind it. Driver and cart shot forward in a flash, and he slowed his pace only when he was approaching the head table and its undisturbed occupants.

Jesuit seminarians had little access to the daily newspapers of Granada. To fill the vacuum left by this lamentable condition, Miguel Agustin Pro began editing his own. He called it the "Scandal Sheet" and he edited it with the consent of his superiors. Since he knew words and phrases of no fewer than five languages, his short articles had something for everyone. Popular subjects for satire were the students or the subjects then being studied. Cartoons which Miguel Agustin drew for his publication were his masterpieces. One famous drawing showed a whole multitude of graceful angels dancing deli-cately on the tip of a needle. At that time, the professor of philosophy was explaining that angels could not dance on or with anything because they had no bodies, but in his vivid imagination Miguel Agustin could picture them and put them down quite amusingly on paper with a few flourishes of his pen.

One of the professors had a peculiar mannerism of puckering up his lips while he thought of the next point he wished to make in his lecture. With his lips formed in this way, he unconsciously made little noises or vocalizations that amused his students. A perfectionist in every way, he had the misfortune one morning of calling upon Brother Pro to recite at the front of the class. With prompt obedience, Miguel Agustin strode up to his place, turned to face his friends and struck the exact pose of his teacher. He launched into his recitation with vigor, using all the mannerisms of his teacher, even to the details of the puckered lips and the strange, singsong noises. The professor was puzzled by the chuckles that erupted here and there throughout the room in mirthful spasms. Finally, it was perfectly evident to him that Miguel Agustin was mimicking him and doing it very well. Brother Pro was ordered to his seat and the class was dismissed without another word. The professor hurried to the office of the rector to demand a penance for young Pro. For three days afterward, Miguel Agustin could be seen at each of the meals kneeling for some minutes in the middle of the dining room floor. He did not appear for recreation during the same period. He freely admitted his guilt and took the punishment that he deserved. At heart, he was a very humble and honest man.

Scolded and corrected for having gone too far with his Mexican gift of mimicry, he said with touching simplicity,

"Don't blame Mexico for this characteristic of mine; blame me. It is typically Pro."

Father Bayle, a teacher of rhetoric, was dearly loved by his students, including Miguel Agustin Pro, but at times the assignments Father gave seemed a bit unreasonable. One day, for example, he demanded that all of Cicero's *Pro Milone* oration be memorized. A groan of anguish greeted this announcement, but he paid not the slightest attention to it. Once work was assigned, it had to be done. Apparently the results of memorization of the long Latin speech were negligible because Father Bayle winced in disgust as one after another of the scholars stumbled through it, forgetting whole passages. "At the end of this term," the disgruntled professor cried, half-seriously and half-humorously, "there won't be enough handkerchiefs in this house to dry the tears you are going to shed when you take your final examinations! You are not studying hard enough!"

A nervous titter passed through the class, but bright-eyed Miguel Agustin with his penchant for remembering little things never forgot that prediction. Months later, he crept into the classroom on the day of the final test to perform a special mission. When he had finished, he tiptoed out and closed the door softly behind him.

Later, when the students arrived, each of them found a large, white, neatly folded bed sheet lying on his desk Attached to it was a small note written in elegant penmanship: "Shed all your tears on this sheet, please!" With all that linen in which to cry, the seminarians would need no extra handkerchiefs.

Brother Pro's fellow students were more susceptible to his playful attacks than his teachers were. One of his companions had a peculiar way of saying, "Yes?" in a high, shrill voice. A feast day was approaching on which music would be performed in the dining room after the gala dinner. For this very special occasion, composer Pro sat down and made up a little song that began on a single high note with the word "Yes?" With his completed masterpiece before him and a choir of fellow conspirators following his expert direction, he rehearsed the song. What the little tenor did not know was that the rehearsal was not going to be at all like the final, formal performance of this work of art. On the day of the feast, each member of the chorus had been told ahead of time to stop at a given place in the music. Sure enough. At precisely the right moment, every voice in the resounding choir stopped singing, and the poor, lonely brother sang out for the whole refectory to hear his penetrating, shrill "Yes?" It sounded so much like the crowing of a rooster that the whole place laughed heartily.

The narration of such insignificant incidents from his student life in Granada should not obscure the fact that Miguel Agustin Pro did work at his lessons seriously and diligently most of the time. In languages, literature, philosophy and moral theology, he was a better-than-average student, according to the testimony of his contemporaries. In dogma, one of the dullest subjects of the curriculum, he acquired only average grades. Running deep and silent beneath his scholastic work, his daily chores and happy recreations, was his spiritual growth in virtue, which he kept hidden from all but his confessor, his spiritual director and his closest friends. Only those who did not know him well considered him to be a light and superficial person. To his close friends, he was an excellent religious who observed the rules and showed exquisite charity to others. Even those on whom he played his spontaneous tricks were the first to laugh as they fell into the trap set for them. And after a good laugh, they invariably came to know and love him more. His exuberant moments at recreation usually followed particularly bad news received from Mexico. In this way he helped his fellow exiles forget their sorrows for the moment, and he was able to ease some of his own pain at the same time. Only rarely did he receive letters from his loved

ones so far away. The messages tore at his heart, for thinly
veiled below the bland surface he could perceive the harsh
truths of privations, uncertainty and anguish from which his
beloved family, friends and country continued to suffer.

Although Brother Pro was not always a brilliant student,
he worked willingly at his books. His superiors were satisfied
with his intellectual, spiritual and social development. With
deep wisdom and correct insight, they knew of his intense
interior life well hidden behind the facade of banter, tricks and
laughter. They were convinced that one day he would return to
his country to help the poor working class falling more and
more prey to communistic influences. As a priest, he would
bring Christ's message and life to them in their poverty and
need. And who but God could know his glorious future? One
of his classmates in Granada, Father Francisco Mateos, was
one day to see a photograph of Miguel Agustin Pro standing
before the firing squad. The thought that sums up so much
instantly sprang to his mind. "He has given to God and to the
Church more glory with his death than all of us with our
profound studies."

Profound studies were certainly not Miguel Agustin
Pro's forte. After his second year of philosophy, he failed the
final examination and had to continue poring over his notes
and books until he finally conquered this high and formidable
hurdle in his scholastic track. But if Miguel Agustin was no
shining light in the classroom, he more than made up for this
deficiency during recreations and vacations. He liked to dra-
matize different scenes for the amusement of his companions.
His best interpretation was that of a motion picture. Using his
wonderful gift as a mimic, he would give his own inimitable
imitation of a new film being projected in the recreation room
on a feast day. Of course he played all the roles in the "filmed"
version he chose to improvise at the moment. But without
warning, he would stop the flow of words and the very gesture

he was making in a silent, frozen position for some moments. When asked for an interpretation of this antic, Brother Pro interrupted his performance to explain.

"Every time our community is shown a film," he said with a wry smile, "it is a rule that the projector must stop somewhere because of mechanical failure." His friends understood immediately and laughed. At that time, before the advent of self-threading motion-picture projectors, one of the most irritating and sometimes hilarious parts of a showing was that in which the film suddenly got stuck in the machine. Sometimes the hot lamp burned a hole in it, or else the seminarian operating the projector managed to shut off the light and rethread the film before sending it whirring again. Meanwhile, the audience waited for the next mechanical failure, which was never long in coming.

The recreation room was not the only stage for the rather extensive dramatic talents of Brother Pro. Sometimes instead of going on a hike for their daily exercise, the young scholastics were sent to the garden to gather vegetables or to pull tall, musty-smelling weeds. On such days, work never began seriously until after the arrival of the popular Mexican. Costume, dialogue and timing were always riotous and fitting for the occasion. During his second year at the Jesuit house of studies in Granada, Brother Pro signed in as one of the charter members of the mission club. At the first meeting of this society dedicated to promoting missions of the Church around the world, the moderator announced that the country of China would be the center of discussion for the day. One of his bright-eyed companions thought it a great idea to sing the Chinese national anthem. It was a beautiful thought except for one thing. Not a single seminarian in the house knew either the words or the music. That of course did not hinder Miguel Agustin Pro in the least.

"You find the music for me," he suggested to a companion adept in composition, "and I'll take care of the lyrics." At first neither music nor lyrics progressed very well. One crumpled sheet of paper followed another into the nearby wastebasket until the lyricist came up with the perfect title: *"Ching, Fou Chang!"* Blessed with such a heading, the poetry and the music followed rapidly, like two mighty rivers merging and plowing their way to the sea. An hour passed and the masterpiece was finished. Miguel Agustin, the new Chinese poet, was the hero of the house. Never had such a work of art been completed in so little time. Never was a national anthem sung with greater vigor by an appreciative audience. So great was the success of the enterprise that even the provincial heard of it. On the following day, he received a letter requiring immediate reply. Unfortunately the author had written his return address only in Chinese. The translation would be simple, thought the venerable provincial. Brother Pro knew Chinese well enough to write a lilting lyric in that language. A simple address would be no trouble at all for him.

Dismayed at receiving the message and letter, Miguel Agustin gathered his friends around him and put them to work. "All the Chinese words I know," he admitted candidly, "are those I learned from a Chinese gentleman in Mexico. The only trouble with them is—they are not good words!"

Assisted by his comrades who poured over dictionaries and maps, he finally managed to translate the troublesome address and went off in triumph to deliver it to the provincial. It is known that Miguel Agustin Pro spoke Spanish with great fluency, French with some facility and English salted with slang phrases indigenous to the United States. His talent for Chinese was and remained extremely limited, and after his harrowing assignment from the provincial, he was never again asked to use his limited vocabulary. One of his most endearing qualities was the ability to laugh at his own failures and the self-set snares into which he sometimes inadvertently fell or entangled himself.

During the years of his stay in Granada, his health deteriorated considerably. His stomach was the source of the pains and discomfort. Yet he never troubled others with complaints about his affliction. Only his close friends knew of his condition and when they tried to sympathize with him, they noted that he quickly changed the subject. Once he pretended to chew and swallow paper wads to prove that his stomach was stronger and healthier than theirs. One day, Brother Escalante noted that Miguel Agustin seemed to be suffering more than usual and remarked about it in an unctuous manner. His friend was irked but made a joke of the whole incident. "Yes," he admitted, "I feel just terrible! My stomach hurts me, and also my kidneys, liver and heart. In addition, even my spleen is acting up. And my head, eyes, nose and throat are beginning to ache. There are pains in my chest, arms, hands, feet and even in my fingernails! You see, Brother, I'm almost at the point where they'll bury me!" Needless to say, after that rather extensive if inaccurate physical diagnosis, Brother Escalante offered him no further sympathy, nor did he soon again inquire into the state of his witty friend's health.

But if Miguel Agustin ignored his own ill health, he tried to cheer his companions during their occasional illnesses with carefully drawn get well cards. Adept at caricature, he drew deftly and cleverly with pen and ink, coloring in details with pastel water colors. From his youth, he had the habit of commemorating events, congratulating the fortunate and consoling the unhappy with witty cartoons. For example, his sister, Ana Maria, treasured two cards he drew for his brothers, Roberto and Humberto. One shows a cat gazing around from a door winking wickedly at a bewildered dog. Another shows a clever young man being tossed on his head from his saddle. His clumsy horse did not quite make the jump over the fence. The horse looks mournfully at his rider, its front legs collapsed beneath its husky frame, its hind legs hanging helplessly over the top fence rail. On feast days, Miguel Agustin found more serious subjects for his pen. He seldom signed anything he drew. He did not have to. Everyone in the house of Granada knew the source of the cartoons.

When an epidemic of influenza swept through the big community of about 125 religious, Miguel Agustin asked to help nurse his friends. Knowing that he did not enjoy good health, his superiors were hesitant at first to grant him permission. However, when more and more of the seminarians fell ill and went to bed, they allowed Brother Pro to work in the separate wing of the building to which the sick were confined. At any time of the day or night, he could be seen making the rounds of the wards performing his chores. So few were those who were well enough to nurse, he was frequently at a window beckoning to his healthy companions below to come up and help him. If they could not recognize him from that distance, he would open the window and pretend he was playing his guitar. That was all he had to do to make himself known. Exhausted from lack of sleep, he finally fell prey to the flu and reluctantly went to bed while others came to care for him.

Even when he enjoyed reasonably good health, he busied himself in small chores to make life in the big college more pleasant for others. Generous, sensitive and observant, he helped put the recreation rooms in order, arranged chairs before classes began each morning, set tables in the dining room and felt perfectly at home with a broom or mop. Always fond of children, he enjoyed going regularly with a companion to the little towns in the valley below Granada to teach catechism. His pupils were not well educated, nor were their parents. But with his knack of communicating with working people and his jovial, openheartedness, he was soon their friend and their long-remembered teacher. He was able to explain the most profound doctrines of faith to youngsters. He used simple terms they could understand at once and plain examples from their own limited experiences. Like the Pied Piper, he attracted swarms of children about him and led them wherever he wished. Nor was his influence confined merely to the young.

One day the children of a village were preparing for their First Communion. As the last of the youngsters trooped into the church to the accompaniment of warm organ music, Miguel Agustin noticed the men of the families loitering in the plaza.

"Don't they go to Mass?" he asked, frowning.

"No, never," was the answer.

Brother Pro turned at once and walked resolutely toward them, his cassock flapping out from his legs as a dusty breeze snapped at it. With a loud joyous greeting, he introduced himself to the lounging men and promptly ordered them to follow him. One looked at another, disconcerted over such an invitation, but they reluctantly obeyed, sheepishly entering the church, hats in their hands, for Mass.

Not on every occasion did Miguel Agustin enjoy such overwhelming success in his humble ministry. Once while walking down a narrow village street, he was greeted by some children who cried: "The priest! Cra, cra, cra!" In his flapping black robe he reminded them of a crow and they jeered at him.

Never outdone in imaginative tricks, he stopped in the middle of the street, turned slowly around to face his assailants and pulled a pack of holy cards from his pocket. He looked directly at one of the small boys and asked, "Do you see this? Do you want a beautiful picture?"

For a moment, the boy hesitated, but thinking he would have the best of the bargain, he came slowly forward with hand outstretched for the enticing gift. Silent and perplexed, his companions watched him move toward the black figure.

Miguel Agustin smiled encouragement to the boy as he inched closer. At the moment the small hand was within range, he pulled the card back, slipped it into his pocket and grabbed his prey. Holding the startled child by the ear, he gave him three good slaps on his chubby cheek saying with each, "Cra, cra, cra!"

The other children jumped to their feet at once, clapping their hands in delight and praising Brother Pro. He had outwitted their leader and had now become their hero. Surrounded by them, he went off in their midst chattering with them. He learned their names, asking where they lived and quickly winning their confidence. Afterward, these children brought their parents with them for catechism lessons, and each week the class swelled in size. The young teacher was so entertaining that he could hold their interest and attention for hours. The women of the town who did not know his name called him simply, "Outstanding Father," not realizing that even though he wore a cassock, he was not yet a priest. "He is the one we like the most," they told their friends. "He simply enraptures us when he teaches."

Brother Pro's rector at Granada during his five years of study there echoed the opinion of the village folk. "He was not very good in philosophical studies," Father Valentin Sanches, S.J., recalled years later. "On the other hand, the Lord had given him a great talent to entertain his neighbors. His expansive and jovial character made him familiar to all, even among the most humble. His never-ending imitation of characters was going to be very useful in time of persecution to hide himself, to introduce himself everywhere, and to do all for all in order to gain them for Jesus Christ. In this he seems a legitimate successor of our [Jesuit] martyrs who in the sixteenth and seventeenth centuries were the most skilled defenders of the faith in similar circumstances to those in Mexico in the time of [President] Calles.

"His virtues? I was his rector and in his soul which he showed me without reserve, he disclosed his admirable patience in the midst of great trials. The bad news from Mexico and the misfortunes of his family hurt him deeply but they did not disturb the serenity of his soul. His fraternal charity was exquisite and never upset. He was always ready to give his brothers his most humble services, to console them in their sorrows, to amuse them with his innocent jokes, especially during vacations."

Having completed his fifth and final year of philosophical studies, Brother Pro began packing his few belongings in preparation for a long ocean voyage. Young Jesuit seminarians usually spend two or three years in the middle of their studies for the priesthood teaching in one or another of their many schools. Mexico was closed to Miguel Agustin and to Catholic education in general, even though Carranza was now dead, betrayed by his former friends. President Obregón held the reins of government. His antipathy for the Church boded ill for Mexicans thirsting for full freedom to practice their religion and for Catholic schools in which to educate their children. So Miguel Agustin was told to leave Granada, Spain, and sail to Nicaragua, in Central America. There he would take up duties as teacher and prefect in a school for boys. Having finished his packing, he gazed around his room for the last time, hoisted his bundles and boxes out into the hall and closed the door on a room and period of life to which he would not return.

The room which he occupied during his long stay in Granada was later to be converted into a chapel. There his old companions hung his photograph on the wall with an inscription to recall to visitors the memory of the beloved martyr. It was preserved there until the day in 1937 when the Communists of Spain attacked and looted the college.

Chapter Seven

The sprawling city of Granada lies languidly on the northwest shore of the vast Lake of Nicaragua. Steaming under a fiercely hot, lemon-yellow sun, it struggles to hold back the jungle crushing in upon it in a green grip of trees, vines, undergrowth and orchids. When exiled from Mexico, the Jesuits decided to build a school for boys there. To this still unfinished structure that Father Crivelli, S.J., had built practically with his own hands, Brother Miguel Agustin Pro came in 1920. Besides the heat and humidity that greeted him like a hot blast of bad breath, he found swarms of mosquitoes and other insects. Occasionally a snake slithered into one of the dormitories to find a pleasant resting place for itself between the cool sheets of a bed. In the tropical climate, such things were commonplace. What required more time to adjust to were the boys who came charging into the school for their first day of classes. It was the first year that boarding students had been admitted to the school. Since neither the boys nor their prefects, the Jesuits, knew much about such artificial living together, problems soon arose.

Brother Pro's tasks included teaching day students, boarding students and small children in the lower grades. Discipline was not easy to maintain among the jabbering, freedom-loving boys who had never before been subjected to serious study or confinement to one building for long hours. Every rule was questioned; every command resented. Gone were the days when Miguel Agustin's mere presence in a Spanish street was enough to gather flocks of children for lessons and stories and games. But in spite of handicaps and the undocile spirits of his new charges, Brother Pro went quickly to work preparing his lesson plans. He taught his subjects vigorously and helped the young boarders overcome their first pangs of homesickness by organizing games for them. Each afternoon under the boiling sun, he was seen running, shouting and jumping in the midst of the boys. Baseball, soccer, tag and games that he made up on the spur of the moment helped the boys forget their loneliness for a while and gave their excessive vitality full scope and direction.

Bats, balls, catchers' masks and sturdy baseball gloves were in short supply when Brother Pro arrived. Undaunted, he organized raffles and bazaars to raise money for the equipment. Young boys soon had toys to play with, while the older students were outfitted with new equipment for their afternoon games. The lively Miguel Agustin continued to amuse his young friends with practical jokes, but these were looked upon with stern disapproval by some of his fellow teachers. At times, even the boys criticized him. His umpiring of a game, they said, gave the other side all the advantages. His assignments for the next day's class were too long. No one in his right mind would be playing baseball at one o'clock in the afternoon when the heat is greatest in Nicaragua. Nothing pleased some of them most of the time. Before long Brother Pro realized that his stay in Central America's Granada was not going to be very pleasant for him.

Yet he did the best he could. Although exhausted from teaching and supervising recreations, Miguel Agustin frequently volunteered to help out a fellow teacher whom he noticed was not feeling well. Pains from stomach ulcers continued to plague him periodically, but he hid his suffering under a veil of good humor. He never mentioned that he was having troubles of his own. Late in the afternoon, when his regular work of the day came to an end, he made his way to the quarters reserved for the servants. There, as the pink dusk settled over the house and a cool breeze eased itself through the open windows, he gathered the illiterate servants around a table. Patiently he taught them to read, to write and to solve simple problems in arithmetic. Happily helping the workers, he always felt at ease in their presence. His exquisite thoughtfulness and charity in helping them to improve themselves would not soon be forgotten.

Like many other religious communities, the Society of Jesus contains two types of religious: priests and coadjutor brothers. Priests and seminarians studying for the priesthood are assigned the tasks of teaching and supervising. Coadjutor brothers who are not ordained spend their time at manual labor, office work and other necessary tasks around the house. Miguel Agustin Pro always had a special attachment for the brothers of his community. He was never too busy to lend them a hand when the need arose. Once when the brother who rang the bell to announce community exercises became ill, Miguel Agustin replaced him. He rose from bed early every morning for months to clang the bell and with a loud voice proclaim the praises of the Lord, urging them to get up.

During his second year in Nicaragua, Brother Pro was named prefect of the older boarding students. Now, besides his regular classes and supervising recreation, he had to be available twenty-four hours a day for any eventuality. Homesickness, bruises, failure in examinations, pranks, cigarettes smoked in secret and angry fist fights claimed his attention, decision and action with exhausting regularity. Even his sleep was disturbed, although he seldom slept soundly because of his stomach pains. Sick boys came for medicine. Sleepwalkers had to be led back to bed. Boys who screamed from nightmares had to be quieted. With rare insight and common sense, Miguel Agustin counseled the young men and by his example did much to inspire them and lead them to good habits. But there were times when he was depressed at seeing meager results from his constant labor. Then he would seek help and advice from his confessor and spiritual director, Father Portas. This kindly old priest always helped him regain his peace of soul. He encouraged him and urged him to do the humdrum tasks and face the ever recurring problems patiently, since they were God's will for him at the moment. Miguel Agustin was never to forget his confessor's kindness, and later he would write to him as a close friend and confidant. Nor was Father Portas to forget his young disciple. Shortly after Miguel Agustin's death, he gathered many of his letters and had them published in Mexico to encourage the persecuted Christians suffering so many privations from an irreligious government.

Brother Frias was another good friend of Brother Pro during his years in Central America. Blessed with a kind heart and remarkable talent to paint in oils, he fascinated Miguel Agustin with his excellent pictures. Later Brother Pro would write to him describing an art gallery in Brussels: "What paintings! What life and what honesty! I don't say they merit just one, but many bursts of applause. And I give this applause to them in your name. Whenever I see a picture, I say to myself, if only Brother Frias were here so that he could teach me the joys of art! But I myself, poor miner from Zacatecas, do not know how to appreciate the beauty that such beautiful pictures represent. Later on, up there in heaven, we will visit together all the art galleries. There, we will see the infinite fountain of all beauty and loveliness. There we will contemplate face to face him who has within himself in a perfect manner the shades, reflections and tones that our brushes are not able to express, and that in him are living, radiant, sublime and infinite."

Even in his letters written in haste, Miguel Agustin Pro displayed a fluency which became more and more refined. When Father Rossi, a priest living in the house, decided to revive a magazine honoring the Sacred Heart of Jesus, he asked the provincial for help. During the annual visit, the provincial called for volunteers and one of the first to offer his services was Brother Pro. Although already overburdened with teaching, counseling and supervising the boarders, he was the only one of several volunteers to keep his promise. He wrote seven or eight articles that were later published. He created fictional letters exchanged between an uncle and his niece, to demonstrate the psychology of a vain young woman ardently trying to overcome temptations to vainglory. An excerpt from one of the articles makes this clear.

My very dear Uncle,

If only you knew what I feel on seeing someone dressed in stylish ruffles and ornaments, or on seeing the hairdos of blondes and hats with flowers and plumes! If you only knew how I have to go against myself so as not to continually stand in front of a mirror, or not to abuse the discreet use of perfume, or not to parade through the streets showing my beauty. Believe me, Uncle, although a young girl may even be ugly—really ugly—she doesn't think she is. She thinks that if not all, at least a large part of beauty is able to be produced by luck and paint. So for that reason she wants to be seen, praised by many, admired by all and even envied. How proud I feel when I go down the street and the young men whistle at me. I listen with just half an ear when they say: "How elegantly she walks! How beautifully that dress fits her." I would give all the treasures of the world for those exclamations and, excuse me, Uncle, I forget everything in those moments—absolutely everything! Even I know that my vanity grows. My estimation of myself increases; my pride and base passions grow and I feel exhilarated. It seems to me that such things and only those are all that this miserable world is interested in.

In another article, Brother Pro's fertile imagination concocted the following scene in which a devout woman arrives at the gates of heaven and is met there by Saint Peter.

"Good day, Saint Peter."

"Good day, daughter. What's your name? Where are you from? How old are you? What else?"

"There will be time for everything, Saint Peter. Please have the kindness of opening this gate for me. I am tired and I want to enter heaven just as quickly as possible."

"Ah, in just a little while. Here one doesn't enter just by wishing to do so. One has to take everything into account beforehand."

"The story of my life? Oh, everything will be taken care of. Certainly I am no saint but I was always a God-fearing woman—pious, recollected, modest—and I even belonged to the League of the Half-Yard."

"The League of the Half-Yard? What's that?"

"A very effective remedy against immodesty in dress. With a half-yard of cloth one lowers the hem of the skirt and one raises the plunging neckline!"

"Excellent! Excellent! Let me go and tell those in charge that you have arrived!"

If during this period Brother Pro could write such imaginative episodes for a magazine, his personal letters to friends were quite different in tone and feeling. To Brother Zaragoza, a companion in flight from El Llano, he wrote with a hint of sadness to congratulate him on the occasion of his taking final vows as a Jesuit.

My dear friend in Christ, Brother Zaragoza:

The news that I have received from there makes me very happy. I am glad the school continues to be so well-directed. I am especially consoled to know that a good spirit reigns in everyone. It is a shame that as far as I can say for myself such good times are not for me.

I suppose that the 15th of this past August you made your final vows. Although late, receive a very strong *abrazo* [hug] from me and my sincere congratulations. I will offer three Communions for your intentions to thank Our Lord and our most loving Mother for such a singular favor as yours. Do you remember that the 15th of August was a very memorable date for all of us living together in the novitiate in El Llano because it was the day of the dispersion? It has for me personally the memory of two other happenings that were very significant: the day I took this holy cassock and the anniversary of my first vows. We must give thanks to our Blessed Mother, the Virgin Mary, for this predilection with which she has guided us—so unmerited on our part. We must pray to her that she will continue to guide us.

How many and what fervent brothers who were living with us then at the time of the dispersion have since been unfaithful to their vocation. But how many graces Our Lady gives to me and to those who follow after her.

Remember the works and humiliations we endured in Zamora, in Guadalajara, in the United States, and in the trips that you and I made together among the Carrancistas and the bandits? In Ixtlan, when we fled with the priest and hid ourselves in the tall corn; in Saltillo, in Texas, etc., etc....

But you have already received the prize in this life. You almost said it yourself. For me, although I have a long way to go, I place confidence in our Mother. She will help me in following my road and she will always help me realize that which you already have [final vows]. Meanwhile, do not stop praying for me that I will be able to prepare myself as God wishes and complete his most holy will in everything.

It is a letter tinged with sadness and haunted by doubts that would recur with greater frequency and intensity as time passed. He doubted that he would be worthy to be accepted for ordination as a priest of the Society of Jesus. His two-year stay in Nicaragua was now over. Unable to visit his family in Mexico, he wrote a postcard to his brother, Humberto, on July 25, 1922, and mailed it from Corinto, Nicaragua. Its cryptic message tells everything. "I have received letters from Mama. I am going to Spain the 28th. My address is: College of Saint Ignatius, Sarria, Barcelona. Regards to all. Goodbye. Miguel."

Having embarked on the *Peru*, Brother Pro and a few of his fellow seminarians watched the city of Corinto slipping away into a blue-gray blur. If he felt anxiety for his uncertain future, he did not show it as the ship plowed south, then east and finally north and west in a great circle to find the Panama Canal. He entertained his friends and introduced himself to his fellow passengers. He even managed to care for a sick Chinese passenger as the twenty-four-day voyage progressed across the blue Caribbean and through the rough, fuming Atlantic. Making his rounds one day, Miguel Agustin stumbled upon a very sick Chinese gentleman. In order to gain his confidence, Brother Pro, now an improvising physician, took the man's pulse, looked at his coated tongue, rolled back his eye lids and finished by prescribing a very strong dose of laxative! The medicine had no effect whatever. So on the following morning "Doctor" Pro prescribed a second dose with the same dismal result. Finally, in despair, he ordered the man to take a hefty third dose. Shortly afterward, Miguel Agustin was delightedly surprised on deck at seeing the gentleman strolling toward him with a rapturous smile.

"I've just cured a Chinese passenger!" Brother Pro announced triumphantly to his fellow seminarians. "If I had come along a little later, I would have been too late!"

Chapter Eight

The *Pero* didn't puff into port at Le Havre, France until early September, 1922. Having passed through customs with their meager baggage, the tired travelers were soon aboard a train bound for Paris. For three days they delighted in sightseeing there. Trying to see everything of interest in such a short time, Miguel Agustin managed to get himself lost at least twice. Knowing little French, he sought directions mostly by graphic gestures and phrases drawn from a potpourri of languages. He visited the small chapel on the Rue Antoinette where Saint Ignatius of Loyola, founder of the Society of Jesus, made his first vows with the six charter members of that community. Brother Pro prayed in the Basilica of the Sacred Heart on the hill of Montmartre. From the breezy Eiffel Tower, he had a breathtaking view of France's capital.

Shortly before boarding the train for Sarria in Spain, he wrote to Roberto, his brother: "I arrived in Paris after twenty-four days of navigation. Paris is very beautiful but not as lovely as I had expected it to be. I have been here three days and tonight I am leaving. Goodbye. Regards. Write."

Sarria, a quiet town outside the Mediterranean seaport of Barcelona in northeast Spain, was to be his home for the next two years. Almost at once he settled down to the serious study of theology and canon law. For a change, his classes and books fascinated him. The subject matter was important and practical for what he hoped would soon be an active ministry among the workers of his beloved and broken Mexico. So busy was he with his schoolwork that his letters were few and brief. To seventeen-year-old Roberto, his brother and godchild for whom he always had a special affection, he wrote in November: "These few lines are sent with the sole object of congratulating you on your examinations and I hope you came out at the very top. With special diligence I prayed to God for you during those days. I hope you'll earn prizes for your final notebook. Now you have to work and provide some income for the house." Later he wrote a short postcard to his brother: "I hope that everyone over there is well. That is what I ask of God every day. You do the same for me. Are you still receiving Holy Communion frequently? When you write to Concha [Sister Concepción] and Luz [Sister Maria de la Luz] greet them. They do not write to me and I cannot write them because I don't know their address."

After some weeks of tedious studies, Miguel Agustin decided that what his fellow exiles from Mexico needed most was a picnic. Permission for such a lighthearted outing was difficult to obtain from the stern-lipped, rigorous Spanish rector. Undaunted, Brother Pro, with his usual efficiency and charm, went about the house proffering invitations and checking with the cook for sandwiches, cookies, cheese and good wine. At a final meeting called the evening before the great event, Miguel Agustin gathered his companions and announced that everything was now ready. "We are lacking only one thing," he explained blandly, "and that is permission to go."

Groans greeted this announcement, followed by unflattering remarks about his inefficiency. These were hurled at him like sharp barbs. With outstretched arms and fluttering hands, he managed to calm down the volatile Mexicans by promising, "I'll go and get the permission myself!" And leaving them, glum and grumbling in the recreation room, he went off to the rector's room for the confrontation.

"Reverend Father," he began coolly, "would you like to give the Mexicans the pleasure of coming with us tomorrow on our excursion? It would make us very happy."

"But I am very busy," the rector said, a bit surprised.

"Oh, I'm sorry. How unfortunate for us! If...."

"No doubt. But tell me, do you have permission for this picnic?"

"No, Father, because we thought if you came with us we wouldn't need permission."

"I repeat, I cannot go."

"Well, then," Brother said, a sad frown spider-webbing across his forehead, "if that causes you too many problems couldn't we go alone?"

Outwitted, the rector sighed, smiled and granted the permission. Miguel Agustin returned almost at a gallop to his waiting companions with the good news. Loud cheers replaced the groans.

One of the Mexican seminarians who enjoyed the hard-won picnic was Brother Francisco Altamirano. Years before in El Llano he had served as guide and guardian for younger religious. More than once he had to go searching for the hidden Miguel Agustin to hurry him to chapel for second Mass. The two were close friends and since Brother Francisco was as good as he was guileless, Brother Pro continued to play tricks on him. For his birthday, Miguel Agustin composed a litany celebrating the virtues of "Saint Panchito Altamirano." Insisting that such a "devout exercise" would merit the pious soul who recited it ample indulgences he began:

Saint Panchito, pray for us.
Collector of holy cards, pray for us.
Model of devotions, pray for us.
Prince of mystics, pray for us.
King of the innocents, pray for us.
Patron of those in trouble, pray for us.
Procurer of ecstasies, pray for us.

Such invocations went on for an entire page before the proper "Oremus" put an end to the list and announced an appropriate closing prayer honoring the "saint" on his birthday.

But if Miguel Agustin would invent the most ludicrous of litanies to amuse his friend, he could also compose a letter of sympathy shortly after hearing of the death of Brother Francisco's father. It reveals much of his kind heart and deep spirituality. He wrote:

I understand the great pain that this is for you, and although a little late, please let me unite with you in this suffering and offer with all my soul my poor prayers. I can see that this test will be for you most painful because of your wish to give your father Holy Communion [as a priest]. But I know your way of thinking and I know that you will offer this new sacrifice to God. I am sure Our Lord has accepted it for the eternal rest of the soul of your father, so Christian and so holy, who is now enjoying the reward of heaven after this life. He does not suffer anymore. He is already in the possession of God who will be our reward and who will repay the very costly sacrifice that he made to God and to the Church of so many good sons [two became priests]. This thought has to be a sincere consolation for your pain that will dry your tears and make them sweeter and cause you to be more resigned.

Although every day I pray to God for your family, in the future I will pray with greater fervor during a

novena of Communions and rosaries so that God will
give you and your family the necessary resignation and
conformity. However, I know that a family so Christian
and so good as yours will always have the grace of God
in the midst of tears and sufferings. I will ask the priests
here for prayers and Masses for this intention.

During Holy Week of 1924, Brother Pro was delighted at
being able to make his annual retreat in Manresa. He was not
far from the cave in which Ignatius of Loyola prayed, did
penance and wrote his famous *Spiritual Exercises* that have
long been the pattern for retreats all over the world. There
Miguel Agustin devoted himself with extraordinary fervor to
these *Spiritual Exercises*. Each night he took the discipline
with such vigor that his companions could hear the lashing of
the little knotted whips while he recited a psalm. Thus he did
penance for his sins of the past year. Before returning to studies in Sarria, not far away, he sent a postcard to his mother in
Mexico. It pictured the holy cave and in his brief message,
Miguel Agustin pointed out the important parts of the shrine.
"I prayed much for all of you," he assured her. "This is a very
holy place. It inspires recollection and prayer." Deeply moved
by his pilgrimage to this birthplace of the Jesuit Order, he
concluded by stating he had seen a cross etched into the rough
rock of the cave by Saint Ignatius during his stay there centuries before.

Sharing with his founder and spiritual father a great devotion to the Sacred Heart, he wrote a glowing letter to Ana
Maria describing the consecration of Spain to the heart of
Christ during the summer of 1924. In a spectacular ceremony,
the king surrounded by his family, ministers and clergy dedicated himself and his subjects to Christ at the base of a tower-
ing statue of the Sacred Heart. "When will we see something
similar in Mexico?" the seminarian concluded. "Pray to God
for your brother, Miguel Agustin."

After two years of theological studies in Spain, Brother
Pro was transferred north to the village of Enghien in Belgium
to finish his preparation for the priesthood. Long interested in
the plight of the working class, he was sent to Belgium to study
during his leisure time the organization of the Catholic worker
movements then blossoming in that industrial area. French
Jesuits had opened their house of studies some fifty years
before in Enghien, and here Miguel Agustin suddenly found
himself like a pebble dropped into a pond of languages, dia-
lects and accents. Some 130 students from fifteen different
countries came together in this house to finish their study of
theology. Brother Pro had to begin the painful and not always
successful task of learning to speak and write French. At the
beginning of his stay in the humid, fog-clogged village, he had
to confine himself to communication in Latin. Even that was
difficult because each of his brothers in religion pronounced it
with the distinct accent of his native land, thus making compre-
hension virtually impossible. In a letter to Brother Campos
whom he left behind in Spain, he urged: "It is enough that you
send to me an envelope and put inside a card written in common Latin; I say common because in vain can it be compared
to mine which was taught by Chona, the house cat, when he
was playful. By the way, they say here that I will be a professor
of language in Rome after a while because of the great facility
I have in Latin. Of course, my Spanish with Latin endings is
the admiration of those who, after five years of fighting it, do
not even know 'musa, musae' (the simplest word in Latin for
song)." He went on to explain that others had the reputation for
being excellent metaphysicians. He also had been placed in
that category of excellence since he was one day observed
talking to himself as he raced through the declension of a Latin
noun! "It is very cool here," he concluded. "I am colder here
than if I were in the Himalayas."

Neither the pains of stomach ulcers nor the penetrating

cold of gloomy winter weather could long repress Brother
Pro's ebullient spirits. Fog, rain, sleet, snow and interminable
gray days only inspired him to write this poem for his friends
in sunny Spain:

>Who is there...great heavens!...
>Who affirms that here in Enghien
>One spends a happy life
>Buried under the ice?
>The clouds whose dense veils
>Cover the town
>And among so many narrow streets
>Not two steps can be made out
>To the passerby who goes on his way
>After bumping into you.
>But if it is so bad outside,
>Within can it be any better in Enghien?
>Ah! my grandmother!... It makes me shiver
>To think of what is coming.
>A strange dinner
>Always with fried potatoes,
>Always with distasteful greens,
>Always with hard dumplings (lead bullets),
>Always with indigestion,
>For the relief of every trouble.
>But all this is diversion
>Compared to the pain
>Of speaking French....

He ends humorously with the wry remark:

>This epitaph of Pro
>Remains engraved in the ice
>Here he lies dead, without light, sun or life,
>A French ranchero [cowboy].

For friendly, corpulant Brother Amozzurrutia, Miguel
Agustin's only Mexican companion in Enghien, he wrote an

elaborate and ridiculous program for an imaginative and never-held celebration of the feast of Our Lady of Guadalupe on December 12th. Part of the public novena to be held in one or the other of their rooms from December 3rd until the 11th would consist of a dinner for six with only the two hungry seminarians consuming all the food. A cockfight would be planned in which the two friends would take the place of the battling birds. No bets over three *riales* would be permitted. During the historic parade, eight floats would be exhibited: Pagan Mexico would feature Amoz (as Miguel constantly called him) quite drunk with a bottle of tequila in his hand with Pro taming a wild bull, represented by his pillow; Conquest of Mexico called for Pro's pulling the ear of Amoz; Mexican Revolution would see Pro in shirt sleeves holding a rifle on his shoulder and a knife in his hand while Amoz would sit in a corner chewing his nails nervously; Mexican Peace Restored promised to feature a gallant Pro strumming his guitar and singing noisily while Amoz, dressed as an Indian woman, would fight off a wild bull and chew gum placidly at the same time. And so it went. Miguel Agustin ended his madly imaginative scenario with "Long Live Our Lady of Guadalupe! Long Live Mexico! Long live her sons, her poor, her drinkers of *pulque* (cheap liquor) and her browbeaters!"

Curious and interested in youth as well as workingmen, Brother Pro once traveled to Brussels to investigate a school run by Jesuits. Nothing escaped his dark, flashing eyes. Later he was to record his impressions on no less than thirteen typewritten pages complete with drawings and illustrations. Teachers, he noted, thought the students spent too much time at games and sports instead of at their books while the prefects insisted that the boys did not have enough physical exercise every day. "Always the same!" Miguel Agustin wrote ruefully. "Each one wants things his own way." Since the students were not regimented into long files for passage along corridors and up and down stairs, they were relaxed, happy and friendly. The school was their second home, and their love for teachers and school delighted Miguel Agustin.

Boarding students had come there from many foreign countries, but the boy who won Brother Pro's heart came from San Luis Potosi in Mexico. Told that a Mexican seminarian was coming to visit, the ten-year-old could hardly wait for his arrival. Together they chatted about the fried beans and tamales they both missed so much. "Ah, my grandmother!" Miguel Agustin later exclaimed, "he touched the most delicate chord within me. He asked me for a medal of Our Lady of Guadalupe, and I, of course, with my tender heart, after hearing him speak of the fried beans, promised it to him. I will send it to him—the only one I have!" Although he could joke about his native food, his stomach was so badly disposed now that he could not have enjoyed it even had it been available to him. And to add to his suffering, he had to endure a kind of "dark night of the soul" which troubled him for weeks during that long, cold, miserable winter. Sad and discouraged, he feared that his superiors would not allow him to be ordained. One by one he reviewed the years of his religious life, especially those spent in Nicaragua and the conclusion was always the same: certainly he would never be elevated to the priesthood. When he could stand the tension no longer, he wrote to his old confessor and director, Father Portas, seeking his advice and encouragement. However, even before a reply could reach him from so great a distance, he learned of his acceptance for Orders. In a jubilant note to Father Portas he announced, "They have given me the Mass!" And to a friend in Corinto, Doctor Castrillo, he explained:

> This year [1925] I shall have the immense good fortune of being ordained a priest. On the 31st of this coming August, I will celebrate my first Mass. Already you can imagine what happiness floods my soul and

with what satisfaction I can communicate it to you. This sublime sacrament will be given to me by Our Lord. He will concede to me the greatest and truly celestial powers to consecrate the most holy body of Christ, to open the doors of heaven to poor sinners in confession, to regenerate through Baptism souls with original sin, and so many other powers that surpass all earthly and perishable honors in this valley of tears.

Such a solemn act requires special preparation. That is why, since I have the pleasure of making you a participant in my happiness, I ask you to pray to heaven for me that I may be assisted in coming to the altar in a less unworthy manner. I trust a great deal in the prayers of others because the more united we pray, the more easily shall we obtain from God that which we desire.

Therefore, Doctor, I shall have you and your very fine family very much present in my mind during my first Mass. It is for me a debt of justice with which I will comply with the greatest pleasure.

While he waited for the great day of ordination, Brother Pro devoted more and more time to learning about the problems and miseries of the workingman at close hand. Granted permission from his superiors, he went to Charleroi in April to visit the mines and talk to the miners. Covered with black coal dust, he refused a quick shower when he emerged from the mine shaft because he wished to stay with his equally darkened friends, the miners. He even stepped into one of their special train compartments to find himself surrounded by sullen, silent socialists for whom Charleroi was famous.

"Do you know where you are, priest?" one of them asked between mouthfuls of a thick sandwich he had pulled from his tin lunch pail.

"No," Miguel said guilelessly. "Where am I?"

"You are with Socialists!"

"Oh, then I have come to the right place. I too am a Socialist."

"What?" the man asked in surprise. "You?"

"Yes," Brother Pro admitted, tapping his forehead with his fingertips. "Only one difficulty bothers me. When we have taken all the money away from the rich, how are we going to keep it?"

The bewildered man had no answer for that and he decided to change the subject by saying, "There are also Communists among us!"

Miguel Agustin was not frightened. "Communists? Oh, that makes me very happy! I also am a Communist. Wait, it's one o'clock. I haven't eaten and I'm hungry. Aren't you going to invite me to share your lunch?"

Confused and disconcerted by this logical man who insisted that each member of the classless society be given his share of the common property, the miner looked from one to the other of his friends. They averted their eyes and looked at the food in their hands or the lunch pails on their thick knees.

"Weren't you afraid when you came into our compartment?" said the man, softening to the friendly seminarian.

"Afraid?" Miguel Agustin asked. "Why should I be? I always carry arms." For a moment, his dust-stained hands rummaged under his shirt and out he pulled a small crucifix with a thread of silver chain attached to it. "These are my arms," he said simply. "With this, I am afraid of nothing." He went on to explain the love Christ had for workers, and when the train pulled into the next station for a brief stop, one of the men stepped from the compartment. He returned with a candy bar which he shared with a grateful and happy Miguel Agustin. As their journey came to an end, each man in the compartment came up to bid his young friend goodbye. Each one shook his hand warmly.

This touching incident only confirmed the confidence which his provincial superior had placed in Brother Pro. Even before sending him to Enghien to study the social conditions of workers and miners, Father Crivelli hoped to place Miguel Agustin after ordination and his return to Mexico in the city of Orizaba, one of the principal centers of militant Communism. Religious training there was practically impossible and the condition of the working class appalling. In writing to the superior general of the Jesuits, Father Crivelli described Miguel Agustin as follows:

> Brother Pro is now studying theology in Enghien, Belgium. I sent him over there so that during vacation he could give time to the study of social questions. In truth, Brother Pro is not a man of extraordinary talent, but certainly among those sent there he is the most practical. He is a good religious and he was, I should say, born to be dedicated to the worker. He has asked me for permission to live and work with the workers during vacations. Of course, I leave the decision in the hands of the superiors in the college in Enghien. I hope his petition will be granted. The young Fathers of our province who are being formed to handle social problems will constitute a nucleus of directors who will be able later to form others. But this stupendous project cannot be taken to its conclusion immediately....
>
> [Pro] is popular with the workers and...has a familiar way with them. He knows how to adapt himself to their customs, not only with his homilies but also with his manner of speech that attracts them. He knows how to keep people in good humor and understands them. These people can go to him without embarrassment to ask for help. Here he will work very well, because although most of the Mexican workers are full of evil doctrines, the love of their religion and their piety are still rooted deeply in their hearts.

Brother Pro knew of his superiors' plans for him. He let slip no opportunity to learn more and more about every phase of Christian social action—especially that of the young workers. They were the hope of the future and the source of many fresh, progressive ideas for improving their condition. Miguel Agustin visited factories and steel mills where they worked, hovels and homes where they lived, and even the cinemas and theaters where they went for entertainment. At their yearly meetings, he listened to lectures, joined their discussions and became acquainted with many of their leaders. He was fascinated by the work of Canon (later Cardinal) Cardijn and his *Young Christian Workers,* popularly termed the Jocists from their French initials. Miguel Agustin not only attended the closing session of their first national congress but later wrote to the secretary general for more information. "I would like to let everyone know about the JOC in Mexico and Spain," he explained, writing in French. "I am keeping in touch with some directors there and the information I've sent about your organizations has interested them every much." He asked specific questions about the object, programs and rules of the organization. Promising to visit the secretary personally if possible, he closed by saying: "I think one day the JOC will become the ideal model for all people interested in the social and moral elevation of working youth."

Although he was to contribute little to the JOC in Mexico and never reach Orizaba as a priest for the workers, God had special work for Miguel Agustin to do. Soon he would be an apostle to the sick, the outcasts and the hunted.

Chapter Nine

In rapid succession, Miguel Agustin Pro climbed the steps leading to his long-desired goal, the priesthood. On July 19, 1925, Bishop Rasneur of Tournai conferred the subdiaconate upon him. On July 25, a Jesuit missionary from Madagascar, Bishop Givelet, conferred on him the diaconate. Final examinations closed the school term. Early in August, Miguel Agustin, with his fellow candidates for the priesthood, went off to a villa near Enghien for a much-needed vacation. There on a placid, shallow lake, Brother Pro rowed a boat with great gusto, claiming that the pond was not larger than the palm of his hand. Each day he hiked along the lake on his way to Enghien to pick up the mail for his friends. He also mailed letters of his own announcing the good news of his forthcoming ordination and begging for prayers for himself and his companions. He spent much time in prayer before the Blessed Sacrament, but while swimming or picnicking, he was the usual jovial Miguel Agustin.

Before the end of August, he and his classmates returned to their house of studies in Enghien to make a retreat. On the morning of August 30, robed in white vestments, they processed into the crowded chapel to be ordained priests by Bishop Lecomte of Amiens. Two things clouded the happiness of this day: the absence of Miguel Agustin's family from the ceremonies and the absence of his fellow Mexican, Brother Amoz. He had suffered from an attack of appendicitis and the subsequent operation delayed his ordination for several weeks. In a letter to Father Almaguer and his many friends in Sarria, Father Pro described the memories of his happiest day. After explaining the reason for Brother Amoz's absence, he remarked:

> For me it was a disappointment, because I found myself alone. I was almost isolated on those grand and unforgettable days in which the Lord wished to manifest so admirably the infinite love and pity that he encloses in his divine Heart.
>
> I am not going to tell you what happened within me. You say that these things are felt and not said because there are no words to manifest them. This is true, even truer after one has experienced them.
>
> How am I going to tell you of my thoughts, of the sweet unction of the Holy Spirit that I feel, that I almost touch with my hands? It floods my poor and unhappy soul with the dregs of heaven's sweetness and the joys of the angels. Blessed a thousand times be he who gives such consolations to us and who has chosen and elevated us, in spite of all our resistance, to the highest and most sublime dignity that there is on this earth. Against all my proposals, against all that I was expecting because of my cold and hard nature, I could not impede the day of ordination. The moment came when I said with the bishop the words of consecration while tears dropped in rivulets and my heart beat wildly in my chest. Oh vain and petty human thoughts, which are not worth anything when God works directly in our souls!

But...I just said I would not say anything of that which happened to me and now it seems I have forgotten. Let's turn the page. Those who are now priests will understand me perfectly when they remember their ordination, while the rest who will soon arrive at the altar will see my viewpoint this coming year.

The decoration of the church, the crowd, the music, the ceremonies, already you can imagine it and in part you will see it when I send you the photographs that were taken. I can tell you only that I saw the bishop who ordained me and I did not notice anything outside the ceremonies (which lasted three hours).

After ordination, the new priests went to the reception room to give their first blessing to their parents and relatives. Only four of us did not have this good fortune. Nevertheless, I went to my room; I put the pictures of my family on the table and I blessed them with all my soul. Afterward, I blessed my other sisters in religion who on that day were united with me in spirit and from whom I had received so much good. And finally, my third blessing was for the souls that God had shown me that I might save and among whom I must work.

After a light breakfast (it was now 11:15) we went to the garden to bless the community, to receive the kissing of hands and the *abrazo* [hug]. I began very bravely but at the third encounter I started to feel a lump in my throat that squeezed me too much. I could not hide my feeling when a fourth asked me if my mother had come. May God forgive me.

The rest of the day passed by...I don't know how. I had no head for anything and I went to the chapel to speak with Our Lord because I felt the necessity of unburdening myself. I believe I spent the whole afternoon there—four hours or four minutes—I have no notion of the time.

The night from the 30th to the 31st was like the previous ones. I slept little, daydreamed and did not rest at all. The wonderful day of the 31st came. At six I assisted at the first Mass of a North American priest from Missouri who had no family. I began my first Mass in the chapel of Saint Joseph at seven. My priest assistant was Fatherr Creniault. A Hungarian priest served for me and about a half dozen assisted, among them Father Lima and the priest from Missouri. I took thirty-two minutes and in the judgment of those present, I spoke like an older priest (for I had practiced so much). In the beginning I was a little nervous but after the consecration I felt peace and joy from heaven. I prayed for all of you at Mass with the greatest fervor and devotion that I could. At 8 o'clock I attended another Mass of a priest without a family and after the meal I talked with Father Creniault.

The meal...horrors! Three hours of verses, songs, speeches. Each new priest had his priest-assistant on one side and his father or brother on the other. I had on my left an ancient gentleman, a capitalist from Lille, who cried like a little boy on hearing the compliments to his son. After learning I had no one from my family there, he overwhelmed me with attention and told me he was my father, loved me much, etc., etc. Poor old man! May God repay him for his good intentions.

At five, after benediction, I went for a walk with Father Creniault and this gave me a great deal of relief. During the night I slept well. I dreamed that in the chapel of Cartuja I was giving Holy Communion to my parents and those studying theology in Sarria.

Yesterday I went to the station with my assistant priest and later with Father Lima, who left his house of studies to go to Granada. During the afternoon I went to Brussels to bless and visit Brother Amoz. But as he is in the clinic of the sisters, I don't know what order, I merely say I gave my blessing in every corner, stairs, hall.

Today I went to say Mass in a convent of sisters. I did not have a server but a holy nun...from the depths of the chapel, answered me in a language I did not understand. Tomorrow I will celebrate Mass in Brussels so as to give Communion to Brother Amoz and to attend his operation. If, as I hope, it turns out well, I shall leave on the 4th for Paris. This year I will not be able to carry out my plans in the Popular Action for I have to return on the 14th. I shall do everything possible to celebrate [Mass] in Montmartre, in our Lady of Victories and in the little chapel where our first priests made their vows.

I send regards to each and every one of the fathers and brothers of the college and ask that you do not fail to help me with your prayers by giving thanks to the heart of Jesus for so many favors received. I close, assuring you that I shall pay you back with much charity, recommending you to God in my daily sacrifices and Masses.

To his old friend, Brother Frias in Nicaragua, Father Pro wrote:

God, our Lord, has shown infinite pity to me because in spite of my faults, my imperfections, my sins, he has raised me to the highest dignity on earth. Blessed be he a thousand times! Help me, Brother Frias, to thank him and ask him that I may be a holy priest without putting obstacles in the plans he has for me. With him I do not fear and I shall walk surely wherever holy obedience sends me. A week ago I came to Paris to the Popular Action to orient myself a little and learn of the work for the year.

His days were filled with activity. After Mass, celebrated in one of the famous churches of the city, he spent hours consulting priests of the Popular Action or sitting in their library poring over books and magazines dealing with the worker and his problems. His notebook bulged with the titles and authors of at least two hundred helpful books he hoped later to secure for his library in Mexico. With his own hand he jotted down notes on everything from labor unions to Communism. For example, he wrote:

> We should persuade ourselves with humility that we are the leaders in the name of the Church not only in religious matters but also in social questions. We should form our opinions to widen our horizons, to look toward the future, working always for the honor of the Church. We should not limit ourselves to a narrow ministry. The priest who contents himself with working for some few souls may be well-intentioned but he has the spirit of a sacristan. Let us imitate our father, Saint Ignatius, who was a true revolutionary, a renovator, an innovator in the good sense of these expressions. He suffered many imprisonments because of his sermons and doctrines filled with new ideas.

With his deep love of country, Father Pro was still fully aware of its faults. He noted: "In Mexico the intellectual level is rather low, and should be raised. Because of this it is necessary to form the clergy, the faithful, the workers to prepare an elite, to study, to pray...." And with a vision far ahead of his time in social matters, he wrote: "Learned people are afraid that the Church does not pay attention to things of importance. The Socialists are more interested in the fate of the workers than we are. The popular masses know this; they can see it and from there the consequences can be drawn. We ought to talk, to shout against injustices. We should have confidence and we should not be afraid. We should proclaim the principles of the Church, the kingdom of charity, without forgetting that of justice as sometimes happens." And if he could see the weakness and faults of the country and Church he loved, he was equally clear-sighted about Communism. "The Communist," he insisted, "has a brutal sincerity. He is moved by savage hate and he is ready to spill blood on the altars of triumph." Knowing the effective techniques used by Communists to dominate men, he studied the same techniques used by the Jocists to help and liberate workers. After his return from Paris, he traveled to Brussels to spend a week with priests and workers of the Jocist movement at lectures, discussions, meals and prayers. He wrote describing this event:

> I made myself a friend of the workers. I met about one hundred of them. I spent recreation time with them and chatted in the interludes between lectures. One of them, a young man of sixteen, who did not have a companion from his town, didn't leave me in sun or in shade. He got up before the rest to serve my Mass. He sat at my side during the discussions, the meals and the lectures. Even when I was saying my Office, he walked silently beside me. I'm losing my mind with this worker! In the toasts at the dinners (we were eating together) they made a nice remark about me and they took me for nothing less than the delegate from Mexico.

Honored for his interest in their work, Father was hailed as the Mexican Jesuit Director of Social Work.

At the close of the congress, Father Pro returned to Enghien to begin his last year of theological studies. During vacations he hoped to exercise his priestly ministry in French cities harboring large colonies of Spanish-speaking workers. His plans for study and the ministry were soon interrupted, however. Early in November, x-rays of his "interesting stomach" revealed a massive, bleeding ulcer. On November 17 he was wheeled into the operating room of Saint-Remy hospital in Brussels to have a large portion of his stomach cut away and the little that was left cauterized. The days that followed were full of pain, lack of sleep and patient prayers. In a letter to his mother, Miguel Agustin was able to explain the operation by drawing illustrations of his digestive tract before and after surgery. By Christmas he was ready to return to Enghien, but a hemorrhoid came to trouble him, and on January 5, 1926, he underwent an operation for this. Pain was now his constant companion. Unable to digest food, bleeding freely from the stomach incision that stubbornly refused to heal, he endured the long days and sleepless nights of convalescence with wonderful patience. The nuns who staffed the hospital and his fellow patients of the ward enjoyed his company, but deep inside, this smiling, young priest was troubled. His year of theology was all but lost. His ministry was practically nonexistent. "This past month I've celebrated only seven Masses," he lamented in a letter. "After the first operation I missed saying twenty-one." Before he entered the hospital he had said, "I am not afraid of physical sufferings," but the spiritual trials were even more difficult to bear. It was especially difficult not being able to celebrate Mass so soon after the powers of ordination had been granted him. In the middle of February, he consented to a third operation to discover why the old wounds refused to heal. Cauterization was used in an attempt to close the scars. A strict diet had to be followed, and more endless days were spent in bed while Father Pro pored over his theology books. "Blessed be God for everything," he told those who came to comfort him. "He knows the reason for these misfortunes, and I resign myself and kiss the hand that makes me suffer so much."

Probably the greatest suffering of this period resulted from the news of his mother's death. He wrote to Father Cavero:

> At noon on the 10th of February, I received a cablegram telling me that on the 8th my mother died. Providentially, I had received a letter two days before that had prepared me. However, the letter did not tell me that cancer of the stomach with complications in the

liver and heart had destroyed all the doctor's hopes of saving her life. This letter was dated January 16. It was a hard blow. My only illusion of returning soon to Mexico to give Communion to my little mother vanished. I spent all afternoon of the tenth almost insensible. During the night, having the crucifix as my only consolation, I cried much. You know, Father Cavero, how one cries for a mother. But in the midst of my pain, I felt an immense joy, a very great interior consolation, and a profound conviction that my mother did not need my prayers—that she was enjoying God and was happy for all eternity. In that hour I felt as if my mother were at my side, as if she hugged me and blessed me. I felt that she was consoling me, making me raise my eyes and heart to heaven where God disposes all things for our good.

And you will understand what my feelings were at Mass the following day: a son who offers for his mother the most pleasing and acceptable Victim, the only one that takes away the sins of the world. Believe me, Father Cavero, I really hesitated, wondering whether to offer the Mass for mother or for my family. Such was and is my conviction that she already enjoys God. How fortunate she is! How many graces she will obtain from God, for my sanctification, my ministry and my studies. She will watch over her sons who are now left alone in Mexico. I am asking her to obtain my recovery from the heart of Jesus.

To friends who had sent letters and prayers, he wrote: "Thank you, thank you very much for your prayers which have kept me from taking a revolver and cutting the thread, not of my life but of that which kept me in this holy hospital or prison of Saint-Remy. That does not mean that I am now well but that I am terribly bored. Blessed be God who in this way gives me a part of his cross which, because of my impatience, will not be completely meritorious."

Late in February, he wrote of his plans to Father Cavero: "Within eight or ten days I shall be able to travel and, if Our Lord permits, I shall go to spend Lent with another sick priest in a rest home or sanitarium near Marseilles (on the French Riviera). I protested because of the expenses and my theology course. However, Father Rector told me it was not for me to plead my case but for him to tell me what I ought to do. So be it! My fate is in the hands of the Lord."

Having said goodbye to the nursing nuns of Saint-Remy, Father Pro made his way to southern France where he was welcomed by the Franciscan sisters into the Villa of St. Mary of the Angels in Hyères. There he said the first Mass each morning so that the other priest-patients could sleep later. "It is no sacrifice for me," he explained, "because I can't sleep anyway." Insomnia, his constant companion during his months of hospitalization in Belgium, had followed him doggedly to southern France. After finishing his own Mass, he insisted on serving the Masses of the other priests throughout the morning. "I only wish I could serve all the Masses that are celebrated," he insisted fervently when told he had been sent to the Villa to rest and recuperate, not to exhaust himself.

He spent the rest of the day visiting fellow patients. His cheerfulness and jokes brightened their outlook and caused them to laugh, and his kindness and counseling brought about several conversions. Such spiritual success he attributed to the prayers of his mother. "From her heavenly home," he insisted, "she helps to save souls."

Father Pro had to prepare conferences for the nuns. He spoke French, much to their admiration and edification. "I have gone from Herod to Pilate," he groaned in a letter to his friend, Father Quintero. "From nuns in white wimples and black veils I have come to nuns with red wimples and white habits. Here I am, my eyes turned up to heaven, my chin twisted, my neck lowered and my hands joined, forming a new caste of nuns that venerates, admires and blesses me. I preach, in very poor French, in sermons and in conferences in parlor, in the sacristy, or behind the grille, while my wimpled spiritual daughters listen to me with admiration. My words are jealously kept in notebooks of conscience. My advice is discussed in spiritual conferences, and my direction is sought as if it were a philosopher's stone (to change base metal into gold)." And if the conferences were too short and to the point, Father Pro would soon hear about it. "I prefer the scalpel to the chapel!" he concluded ruefully.

The fascinating young priest was soon known to rich and poor outside the rest home at Hyères. "It is 2 o'clock in the morning," he once wrote describing one excursion to a nearby chateau. "Sleep has gone for a walk. Let us imitate it. Come along with me." With that he launched into a witty description of his journey by car to a countess' home where he found himself surrounded by her admiring family and servants. A tour of the house revealed paintings by Rubens and Van Dyck on the walls, a palm tree planted by the poet Lamartine in the garden, a room used by the famous preacher, Lacordaire, and a writing table at which Paul Bourget had written some of his novels. Only three months before, he was assured, the Queen of England had paid a visit to his charming hostess and her husband. All of which simply "finished my stock of exclamations, interjections and expressions of admiration *a là française,*" Father Pro concluded playfully.

"Let us leave the nobility," he continued on a more somber note, "and go down to the commoners in shirt sleeves. I like doing that. I bless God for having conferred upon me the great dignity of being a priest. What wonderful happiness one finds in bringing peace to a troubled workman's family! What joy in taking Holy Communion to a youngster of ninety-four! What pleasure in sitting under a tree and hearing the confession of an easy-living gardener or of teaching the basic points of catechism to a Communist while kicking the shavings and sawdust of his workshop!

"I am now quite sure of one thing: the facility with which I pass from one social class to another is not, as I used to think in my joyous youth, owing to my physical advantages nor to my sound and sweet piety. Not a bit of it! It is all due to the fact that, poor rascal that I am, I belong to the Society of Jesus. The name Jesuit is enough to open up the doors of all types to me. Above all, it is on account of the holy and undeserved grace of the priesthood that God has bestowed upon me."

Hyères, the fine winter resort, was meant to "contribute its tropical sun, fresh breeze, blue sky and pure air to the physical recovery of my demolished and cut-up humanity," Father Pro wrote. But it did little to restore his health during his short stay there. To his friend, Father Campos, who was concerned about his condition, he wrote: "I must tell you what I need so that you can send it by return mail. I need:

"1. Patience. I have been using my own for so many years, it is beginning to get a bit worn out.

"2. Work. The idle life I am living does not go at all well with my character, with my nervous temperament.

"3. An old camel with a hollow on its back which I could use as a chair or carriage on my visits to hospital, clinics, sanitariums, doctors and nurses.

"4. Spirit of faith (if there is no camel to be had) to swallow all the drugs they prescribe for me (because, as you know, castor oil is the only remedy I believe in). Do you think I am joking? Not at all!"

Both Father Pro and his superiors realized that he would never again enjoy good health. Haunted by the thought that he was now useless to the Order and distressed that his superiors were too kind to tell him so, he wrote, "Why don't they speak to me openly? From now on I would offer up my life willingly. After all, God does not need me to do the good he wishes done in Mexico!"

In mid-May he boarded a train for Enghien and during the journey helped save the life of a young Jewish girl. It seems that the priest had long teased the nuns of Hyères by asking for one of their red hoods to wear back to Belgium. In one of the train compartments he found his red hood in a manner he had never expected. Alarmed by shouts for help, Father Pro went to the compartment of some boarding students returning to Paris. There he found a young woman coughing up large quantities of blood. No doctor could be found and the frightened girls milling about were helpless. While the blood continued to flow and the girl's pulse rate slowed, the priest ordered a lemon to be brought. He cut it and squeezed its juice into her mouth. As soon as she swallowed this unusual medicine, the girl began to breathe normally. No more blood poured from her mouth. She opened her eyes and looked around her. When asked by the train master what should be done, Father Pro said quietly, "Do not let anybody come in here, and make these silly people keep quiet about all this." When he returned to his own compartment, he discovered that his clothes were soaked with blood. He was indeed wearing his red hood.

Back at last in Enghien, Father Pro was tormented by inability to sleep, a poor appetite and physical weakness. Studies were out of the question for him and yet he was able to write to a friend soon to be ordained some of his finest ideas about the priesthood.

> There is something in me that I have never felt before. I see everything in a different way. It is not the fruit of my studies nor of virtue more or less solid, and it is certainly nothing personal or human. It comes from the priestly character which the Holy Spirit stamps on our souls. It is a more intimate participation in the divine life that elevates and deifies us. I can assure you that our blessed Lord has deigned to use me as an instrument to do good to others (during these past six

months). How many souls I have been able to console; how many spiritual wounds I have cured. What courage I have been able to inspire in souls struggling with the difficulties that arise on taking up a holier life! Two vocations almost lost have been put on the right road; a seminarian about to put aside his cassock has followed the call of Providence once more with fresh fervor. Obviously I would be incapable on my own of causing such changes. I have only to regard my ways, my temperament, my disposition and my unfinished studies to be convinced of that. If I have been able to do good to anyone, it is quite clear that I owe it to the grace of my priesthood.

Early in June, Father Pro received orders from his provincial to return to Mexico. With little hope of his health ever being restored or his studies finished, his superior was sending him back to his homeland to die among those he loved. But his life and death during those sixteen action-crammed months were to be quite different from anything his superiors, or he himself, could ever have dreamed possible.

Chapter Ten

During his last days at Enghien, Father Pro packed his personal belongings and wrote farewell letters to his friends. Grateful for all the favors given him during his European exile, he promised to pray for his benefactors and begged a remembrance in their prayers and Masses. And to fulfill one last wish, he obtained permission from his superiors to visit Lourdes before sailing home. However, he had no money for the journey, so he sat down to write an old friend in Spain, Father Negra. As a stipend for four Masses which he promised to say for his benefactor, Father Pro asked for fifteen pasetas. This was enough money to carry him to southern France in a third-class train compartment. There he could pray at the grotto in which Our Lady had appeared to Saint Bernadette. By the time he reached Paris, the money was there waiting for him.

His four days in Paris were busy ones. His passport caused him concern because of the title "religious" stamped on it. Belgian authorities assured him that he would have no trouble entering Mexico under such a title. The consul in Paris was not so sure and civil authorities were certain that the

government of Mexico would not want a native priest returning. Mexico was now headed by President Calles, who delighted in persecuting and exiling priests, monks and nuns.
Nothing was done to change the passport. As it was to turn out,
the Mexican officials would not even look at it when he finally
arrived in his homeland.

On the evening of June 16, Father Pro found himself on
the hard wooden bench of a train clattering toward Lourdes.
He had brought no food with him and during the long night
sleep was impossible. He was later to write:

> I arrived in Lourdes at 8:15 in the morning, and
> there I received the special assistance of our Lady. On
> the street I met the bishop's secretary. I showed him my
> papers. He gave me permission to celebrate Mass and I
> arrived at the basilica. When? When the last Mass was
> finished at the main altar. At nine I began mine. It
> lasted longer than usual because the list of people I had
> to pray for was very long!
>
> From the church I went to the grotto. The grotto! A
> little piece of heaven where I saw the Blessed Virgin
> and where she filled my soul with immense happiness,
> intense consolation and divine joy. All this can be felt
> but not expressed in words. Poor Father Pro could nei-
> ther see nor understand, nor was he even aware of the
> thousands of pilgrims who surrounded him. Once, how-
> ever, when I was looking up to contemplate my Mother,
> I saw at the feet of the Blessed Virgin a sick woman in
> her carriage. She was saying the rosary, her arms out-
> stretched forming a cross. What faith and confidence!
> My heart glowed within me, and I began to converse so
> intimately with my holy Mother that my soul seemed
> carried away with joy.
>
> How did I manage to kneel there such a long time
> when usually I can only bear five minutes on my knees?
> I don't know. At 12 o'clock I went to eat. I wrote four

postcards and at 12:30 I was already back at the grotto. Do not ask me what I said or what I did. I don't know anything. Yesterday I was not the same miserable being as other days.

A priest approached me at 3 o'clock and said, "If you stay like that any longer you will faint. I advise you to go to the baths where there is a little shade." Why did he say that to me? What did I look like then? That is another thing I ignored. I only know that I was kneeling at the feet of my Mother and that I felt very profoundly in my soul her holy presence and action.

In the baths I saw hundreds of poor sick people who came hoping to be cured. A Capuchin priest preached after each decade of the rosary. I did as the others did: I sang, prayed, kissed the ground. With my arms outstretched in the form of a cross, I invoked the Blessed Virgin. At 4:50 p.m. I was once again on the train.

So I have been to Lourdes. I did not visit Calvary. I did not see the Gave River. I cannot tell you what shape the basilica is, nor what it encloses. However, it is quite true that I have been to Lourdes! For me, going to Lourdes means meeting my Mother, talking to her, praying to her. My voyage will not be as hard as I thought it would be. The Blessed Virgin has told me that. Oh, my miserable human nature was finding it hard to go back to Mexico. My health is gone, my studies are finished, my poor country has been destroyed by its governors. I will not even have the pleasure of again seeing my mother who gave me life. I weep for her even in the midst of resignation and conformity to God's will. However, my trip to Lourdes has given me fresh courage.

"Yesterday," he told another correspondent, "was one of the happiest days of my life." Father Pro did not forget his benefactor, Father Negra, who had made the trip possible. He thanked him sincerely and assured him that he had offered many prayers for his intentions at the famous grotto.

Another night journey by train brought the exhausted priest back to Paris. On June 21, he was standing on the deck of the *Cuba.* It weighed anchor in the port of Saint-Nazaire and slipped out toward the open sea. On the list of passengers, his name appeared incorrectly as Father Miguel Agustin Apro. He was probably not aware of the error, surrounded as he found himself with four hundred ninety fellow Mexicans out of a total of five hundred twenty-five passengers. Since they were all Catholics and he was the only priest aboard, from the very beginning he was assured a busy voyage. The *Cuba* visited two Spanish ports in as many days before steaming across the Atlantic. As Our Lady of Lourdes had promised, the crossing was pleasant. Upon arrival on July 4 in Havana, Cuba, Father Pro disembarked long enough to mail the following letter:

> Three more days and I shall be in Mexico! Will they allow me to enter being a priest and a religious? I don't know. But I pray and trust. God is always my Father who guides me. I am the only priest on board and I have been received by my compatriots in the most frank and amiable manner. All the difficulties related to the celebration of Mass vanished as if by magic. The First Friday Communion was very emotional for all present. Ladies, gentlemen, children and young people in great numbers approached the Eucharistic table. Three of these young people have received Communion daily and have disputed for the honor of serving Mass. With this I am busy every day. Confessions, consultations, private conversations and some little bit of chess have made my trip very agreeable. Do you remember the fear that the trip caused me? Well, he who calls me to Mexico has given me all the faculties and even all the considerations that a priest could dream of. Help me to give thanks. I do not recall that I have even been sick.

Father Pro arrived in Mexico where the persecution of the Church begun by Carranza in 1914 and continued by Obregón in 1920, had reached its climax under President Plutarco Calles. Providentially, the priest's passport was not checked at Veracruz, nor were his suitcases opened for inspection. In Mexico City he met his provincial and received orders to continue his ministry at the Jesuit church of Our Lady of Guadalupe of Peace on Enrico Martinez Street. He also learned of the new law President Calles enacted to suppress all activities of the Catholic Church. The law was destined to be put into effect on July 31. The bishops of the country with the approval of Rome had decided to suspend all public services in the churches of the entire country, effective the same day that the hated law was to go into effect. Realizing that little time was left for them to practice their religion in public, Catholics flocked to the churches for Mass and the reception of the sacraments. Confessionals were literally besieged, and one of Father Pro's first tasks was to sit hearing confessions from 5 o'clock in the morning until 11:00 and again from 3:30 in the afternoon until 11:00 or 12:00 at night. "It was a triumph," he wrote to a friend, "but an unfortunate triumph. Twice they had to carry me out because I fainted. My poor carcass which has just left behind the soft pillows of the hospital has not yet got used to the hard seat of the confessional." So busy was the frail priest kept that for three months he was unable to write to friends out of the country and then only during his annual retreat on a quiet farm.

As he described his work in the capital, he admitted cheerfully:

> My confessional was besieged as if it were Jubilee time. My delicate advice drew in old ladies, young painted ladies, corpulent gentlemen, smelly drunks. I said to myself, "Once the churches are closed I shall have nothing more to do but to fold my arms: I shall

then be able to rest after these days full of hard work when everybody wishes to go to confession at the same time." But one can't be popular! People long to come and drink in consolation from my lips and receive help and courage in the fight against the devil, the world and the flesh. Whole lines of cars await my poor person to baptize a baby, hear the confession of someone who is dying or marry a brave couple who dare to put themselves in the indissoluble knot of matrimony. And it is clear that what was done in one hour in the church can scarcely be finished in a whole day in spite of everything else.

I have been chosen "Chief Lecturer...." In my pulpit of fire and smoke, I hurled forth burning examples to a group of young people who must then transmit my doctrine to the faithful! And that certainly gave me some gray hairs, for such conferences were the result of my capitalist youth to people of talent and career. They came to me as if with horns, asking questions not only of philosophy but also of morals, sociology, holy scripture, and above all, politics and government.

I gave them the conferences, and I gave them to the public, going from a carpeted parlor to the basement of a wineshop, from the perfumed auditorium to the plainest home of the worker. But that is not all. Many of the well known priests cannot keep up their ministries because they are persecuted. So I have to replace them, going from Herod to Pilate both day and night. Since Father Ambia has gone, a two-week retreat has fallen onto my shoulders. Now, besides my own parish, on Enrico Martinez Street, I have to help at Holy Family. It is as if they had said: "You cannot fight a goat? Well, then have a go at this bull!"

How was I able to resist? How do I resist? I, the weak one, the delicate one, the most recent guest of two

European clinics. I spent my days lying on a divan sipping broths. I hardly ever had to touch my slippers because a thousand nuns disputed the honor of taking them off for me! All this proves beyond doubt that not I, but the grace of God in me, was doing this.

I have what I call "Eucharistic Stations" (in private homes) where I go each day to bring Communion, making fun of the vigilance of the police, some days at one place, other days at another. On an average, I give 300 daily Communions. On the first First Friday I had only 650, the second First Friday 800 and the third 910! That is true. It gives me a terrific amount of work but I keep on going. The work in the confessional is great also among the glittering would-be saints, the scrupulous men. They are the worst, with worldly youth and the silly servants and stubborn boys and the simple children, but all of them worthy of the work of a miserable type like me. They are even worth the apostolic zeal of thousands of missionaries. Our unhappy people are moved to make reparation to the Sacred Heart of Jesus by fervent Communions for the offenses of our wretched government against him.

If only I had time to tell you some of the examples of virtue I see daily. These people, both rich and poor, are touching. My confessional is a real exercise of humility for me when I realize how far I am from imitating those who seek my direction. "Help me with your prayers," as the French say, that my soul may profit by it all.

But will I be able to write again? The revolution is a fact. The reprisals will be terrible, above all in Mexico City. The first to be taken prisoners are those who had dipped their hands into religious affairs, and as for me, I have forced them in up to the elbows! If only I could be among the first or among the last but to be among their

number! If this does come about, prepare your petitions
for heaven because I will be your best advocate. However, honey is not made that way!

Regards to all in this world and in the next.

Having signed the letter as simply the "Miner" to hide his
identity in case the letter fell into the hands of the police,
Father Pro added a postscript: "The censorship of the mail is
terrible. That is why I do not write my name. In another letter I
shall write my address."

On a quiet and secluded farm the priest was able to make
his annual retreat and help a brother of the Society make his.
Shortly afterward his superiors ordered him to go into hiding.
From this kind of prison he wrote to his provincial:

> You know very well that I am not especially in-
> clined to anything in particular, although it is rather
> hard to lose the chance of going straight to heaven or of
> becoming a chaplain of the Marias Islands [where the
> government deported its prisoners].
>
> I prefer to obey, being quite convinced that I will
> thus be of more use to those to whom I wish to dedicate
> my work and life. I have no desire to influence your
> decision, but I would like to follow the advice that
> Father Crivelli sent us from Rome: please let me remain
> at my post until the end of the persecution.
>
> Fear withdraws the priests from their abandoned
> flocks. Now, as you know, fear is not my predominant
> fault. I might die? What they might do or what they
> might do to me—all that is in the hands of God.
>
> Would that I might be found worthy of suffering
> persecution for the holy name of Jesus. Do I not belong
> to his army? But let us repeat as in the Our Father: "Thy
> will be done!"

Released from his hiding place and sent back to active
ministry in the city, Father Pro assured his provincial that he

was doing well, thanks to ample help from the Lord. "The work is hard and continuous," he admitted. "I am lost in admiration at all that the great Chief manages through me. Illness? Pains? Cares? I have no time to think of all this. I am so well and so strong that apart from some very small relapses I could remain well until the end of the world. I am ready for whatever you may dispose, but, if you have no objections, I would beg you to let me continue here while the present crisis lasts. How happy I would be if I could be one of those whom they are going to hang up on the statues of Pegasus in the Zocalo!"

The statues he mentioned were in the great public square of the city where the government saw fit to hang the criminals who broke its laws and, especially at that time, those many devout Catholics who defied Calles' irreligious law.

From his provincial, Father Pro received the order to continue his study of theology during the free time available to him. He was to take the examinations when he felt he was ready for them. In spite of his many tasks and erratic form of life, he was frequently seen studying until late into the night. When books he needed could not be found, he begged his friends to find them for him. During his times of hiding imposed by his superiors, he obediently endured in spite of the boredom and pain they caused him. He always took his textbooks with him and pored over them even though he disliked the task intensely. For a whole year this was to continue. Just two months before his death, he took the examination with good results, considering the difficulty he had in pursuing studies in that troubled time and place.

Although work continued to increase for him, the zealous priest did not lose his sense of humor. Early in his new ministry, he forgot that eggs were a type of food forbidden him by his European doctors. Scheduled to appear as a guest preacher, he enjoyed a hearty lunch of highly seasoned foods he loved.

One of the dishes was an egg omelet. Hours before the sermon was to be delivered, he was writhing upon his bed with an agonizing stomachache, and instead of his climbing to the pulpit to deliver the long-awaited homily, another Jesuit had to replace him. Not only that, but his friend asked the congregation to pray for the recovery of the ill Father Pro. "Thus passes the glory of the world!" he chuckled after his recovery.

Chapter Eleven

Although the work was heavy and the dangers many for Father Pro after his return to Mexico, he had the consolation of being reunited with his family. His brother Edmundo had married four years before and now had a home of his own. Humberto and Roberto had grown to be vivacious, handsome young men actively engaged in the work of the National League for the Defense of Religious Liberty. This famous League made up of zealous young Catholics did all in its power to oppose the anti-religious laws and edicts of President Calles and his government. Old Señor Pro, whose hair had turned white but who still carried himself erect and with poise, was the center of the family with young, pretty Ana Maria to look after him. "We changed houses almost as often as we changed clothes," she remembers, thinking back to those days of their precarious existence. It was in this condition that Miguel Agustin found them. He spent his nights with them because community life among his fellow Jesuits was now out of the question. Churches, shrines and schools were closed by order of the government and all priestly activity was driven underground. Private homes became meeting places for the Mass. When the persecution was raging furiously, Father Pro wrote to a friend:

> Here things are getting on like a "house on fire." Catholics are sent to heaven for any trifle. Anyone who goes to prison is sure of never again sitting down at his own table. My relatives are so well persuaded of this that when they go out, instead of saying "goodbye" they recite an act of contrition.
>
> We know quite well that whoever does not return home by 11 o'clock at night is sure to have served as a target for the bullets of our dignitaries. We have had a family reunion, and we have officially said goodbye to each other until we are united again in heaven. Still, instead of breaking into tears, we broke out in laughter. Don't you think it's wonderful to go straight off to the heavenly mansions for such a noble cause?
>
> What wouldn't I give for you to be able to come and spend a day here with us! We live in a hiding hole, receiving no visitors and with just the necessary things for life. All of this is a loan, although really it is a gift because neither we nor our heirs will return any of it to its owners. But since no goods are necessary to enter heaven, we let it all go cheerfully.

But though the times were difficult and the sufferings and privations great, Father Pro never lost confidence in God. "The splendor of the resurrection is already on its way," he wrote, "because now the gloom of the passion is at its height. From all sides news of outrages and reprisals comes pouring in. There are a great number of victims. The list of martyrs gets longer every day. Oh, if only I, too, could win this great prize!"

Each month the number of Communions to be distributed on First Fridays continued to grow. He wrote to his provincial living in El Paso, Texas:

> Just imagine what this means for a poor little priest

who has no experience in the confessional. Perched on my brother's bicycle, I go down these streets of God like a horse possessed by the devil. I am always in danger of death because the drivers in Mexico are extremely daring.

As far as the other ministries are concerned, I have lost count. The care of the sick is the occupation I prefer and also administering Viaticum and Extreme Unction. Baptisms and marriages are in abundance, too, among the working class. Among the ones I liked best were the baptisms of two young women who were twenty-five and twenty-eight years old. They had made the mistake of receiving Holy Communion before being baptized! Then there was the marriage of a couple who had lived the wrong way for twenty-five years, the conversion of various Socialists and a heretic and very many First Communions. In the poor quarters, going here and there among people of my sort, I am really in my element. I speak, I cry out, I bellow at my audience. The best part of them have no shirt on and they are in danger of being caught by the police when they come to my lectures. Poor people! One can do such a lot of good among them!

To Father Carlos Mayer, the provincial's representative in Mexico City, Father Pro wrote frequently, calling him in secret code, "Señor Carlos." When the police became suspicious of the young man who managed to carry on his ministry in various disguises right under their noses, Father Mayer had to limit Father Pro's activities and at times order him into hiding. Father Pro always obeyed, but he had to admit, "How difficult is the holy virtue of obedience! You can accuse me many of things," he continued, "but you will never be able to say anything about my obedience."

From his cramped hiding place he wrote his provincial in February of 1927:

Obedience is better than sacrifices and that is why I

have not moved from where I am. But permit me to tell you one thing without pretending to criticize or murmur. The situation here is very delicate. Danger surrounds us on all sides. I know very well that God helps those who help themselves, but the Catholics need our spiritual help. Each day that goes by I hear of people dying without receiving the sacraments. There are no priests exposing themselves to the danger. Through fear or through obedience they keep to their hiding places. Helping, by my little grain of sand as I have done up until now, means perhaps exposing myself to danger, but I don't think I would be too rash. I would try to be cautious and prudent. Señor Carlos is more than afraid, I know.

However, I think that between fear and rashness there is a middle course. I have told Señor Carlos all this but he still fears for my life! My life? What does that matter? Would it not mean saving it if I were to lose it for my brothers? Of course one must not throw it away stupidly, but when will the followers of Saint Ignatius enter battle if at the first shot they turn their backs?

I am not boasting when I speak like this. I am well aware of the very little courage I possess but I feel that I could give courage to others, both priests and laymen. After all, the worse that they could do would be to kill me, but that will only happen when God's good time arrives.

When his exile was finally ended and the hours of pacing the floor, studying and praying came to an end, he was hurled into new activity, this time giving retreats in various parts of the city to the most diverse types of audiences. The taxi drivers intrigued him. "They all belong to the type that wears a cowboy hat, has long sideburns and spits on the floor," he wrote describing them. "Good golden pieces in spite of their lack of manners and their dirtiness. To my great astonishment I found that strong words flowed quite naturally from my lips. I thought I had forgotten them all in the sixteen years that have passed since I left the mines but it was just as if I had left them yesterday! I don't need to emphasize the solemnity of these conferences. In a courtyard, I gave them dressed as a mechanic, a cap pulled down to my nose and elbowing my congenial audience. May God bless all the drivers of the whole wide world!"

His next retreat brought him before eighty teachers and government workers. From the beginning, the pretty young women caused their young retreat master to sweat profusely. They did not believe in the existence of God, the doctrine of hell and the immortality of the soul. Undismayed, Father Pro continued his talks and answered their objections. Before ending the retreat he had the consolation of giving every one of them absolution and Holy Communion. Yet for such success he took no credit, realizing that it was the grace of God that had touched and converted these penitents who at first had appeared so hardened and obstinate. "How much misery," he concluded, "because of the lack of religious education!"

At times, he had to preach two retreats at the same time, and between homilies and times in the confessional he was called upon to assist the dying in homes nearby. Had he been three or five or a hundred men as he so fervently desired, he would not have been able to do all the work awaiting him. Shortly before his death he preached his last retreat in Toluca, a town not far from Mexico City. "My work here is simple," he wrote. "It consists in offering my articles [homilies]. In the early morning I offer them to devout old dears, a little later to young ladies, about three in the afternoon to servants, at five o'clock to ladies, at six to my companions, and at night to gentlemen. We will see who will be the best clients." Summarizing his work he said, "I talk all day long but people have responded well. If only my employers would let me travel around the whole of the Republic. I am rather tired, because my sale was more of a clearance than I had expected." The retreatants had gathered in three rooms of a house for the sermons and exercises. Some two hundred men crowded into the quarters to hear the word of God. Although the police were only a short distance from the house, the priest led his hearers in prayers and hymns for three days without being detected or hindered in any way. The response from the men overwhelmed him. A shoemaker assured him that his homilies gave "a great deal of prestige to the morale of the nation"—whatever that meant! And he shook hands with the slender priest with such fervor that Father Pro could smell the shoe polish on his palm for the next three hours.

Through trusted friends, a constant stream of notes went out announcing the time and place of the next Mass, a three-day retreat, a private meeting for counseling, an opportunity for confession. Many of these have been kept by their owners. With spies and police everywhere, his ministry was made all the more difficult and clandestine. Yet even in the midst of his work, he dreamed of founding "an academy of vocations" made up of young men whom he hoped to shepherd to the priesthood. Death came for him before he was able to carry out his plan, but his eyes were always on the future and his hands on the concrete present moment, doing all in his power to help others. By his personal magnetism and example he led at least one boy to the priesthood. His name was Miguel Pardinas, a lively mischievous youth who attracted the priest's attention during frequent visits to his home. Often Father Pro defended the boy after a prank or practical joke, and once he promised the bright-eyed youth five pesos if he would do all of his homework for a month. The bargain proved too much for little Miguel but the priest gave him the money in spite of his lapses. One day Father Pro caught the boy squirting a servant girl with a hose on the patio instead of hosing down the walk. Screams of chagrin and the shower of water stopped abruptly as the priest asked sternly, "Isn't she also a Christian?" The boy was so stunned by the words that he began to cry and ran to the priest and the girl to beg pardon. It was given at once but the boy never forgot the incident. Later he became a Jesuit priest and a famous missionary to China. His love for jokes and his zeal for souls were much like those of his friend and model, Father Pro.

As practical in dealing with impoverished bodies as he was in ministering to sinful souls, Father Pro divided each of his days into three parts. From the time he arose in the morning until nine o'clock he cared for souls. Mass was celebrated in a private home followed by the distribution of Holy Communion to hundreds of people waiting in one or another of his "Eucharistic Stations." These he reached by bicycle, car or bus. As he bounced along from one to the other, he carried the Eucharist in a small silver ciborium over his heart. This vessel can still be seen with his clothes, theology books and portable altar in the museum of the Jesuit printing press called Buena Prensa in Mexico City. In the evening, he heard confessions, preached homilies, visited the sick, offered spiritual direction and finished saying his Office. For five or six hours each day he helped the poor. It was at his "Eucharistic Stations" that he became keenly aware of the need of the corporal works of mercy. By February 1927, his work for the poor was already highly organized. Called the "Center of Charity" and aided by Señora Josefina Nunez de Colin, a small group of men and women formed the core of this movement which still exists to help the unfortunate. Without a penny of fixed income, they filled large sacks each month with coffee, rice, sugar and grain for what began as a mission of mercy to only a few families and quickly grew to a total of nearly one hundred. Rescue missions in different sections of the city cared for the needs of these areas and the surplus of one went on to another in need.

Provisions for a month were laid aside for the "families of God" as Father Pro called his poor people. To have saved more than that would have been to show lack of confidence in God. When his friends said this was foolish, the priest only laughed and countered with, "It is still more foolish to take charge of about a hundred families without any fixed resources."

Food, clothing and even empty houses were obtained for the poverty-stricken. "Nobody knows where I live," Father Pro wrote describing his work for the poor. "I receive letters, they consult me and send me sacks of flour for my poor people at four different addresses. I am experiencing what one reads in the lives of the saints (don't go and take *me* for one of them). I have no idea how or when, but about fifty kilos of sugar, boxes of biscuits, coffee, chocolate, rice and even wine all came rolling in. The Providence of God is so great that just when I am getting a headache trying to decide which wealthy person I can ask for a donation, I find that my storage bin is quite full. The best part of all is that my sacred person does not have to stand in the limelight. I just pull the ropes and other generous people do all the work." But the work was not easy and often Father Pro had to beg personally. "Food comes in abundance," he once admitted, "but, if the truth must be said, at the price of numerous humiliations. You have no idea how humiliating it is to beg—always to beg!"

Although he took good care to see that his poor friends had food, he ate very little himself. Late one evening he arrived at a home to hear confessions. When asked what he had eaten that day, he pulled from his pocket some peppermint drops. Told that he could not go on living like that, he merely shrugged and assured his host that he would have a good meal in heaven.

"The least numerous families are four to six members," he once said, describing the recipients of his help. "Others total up to ten or even twelve. They all have the exceedingly bad habit of eating meals three times a day and with a good appetite, too. If that were all it would be easy, but children of Adam and Eve that they are, they live under a roof for which one has to pay rent. They wear shoes which get worn out and wear clothes they embellish with holes. They even know the art of falling ill and needing medicine!

"Of course one can't always bring sufficient relief to all these necessities, but I make use of my friendship with the doctors who forget to reclaim their salaries. I also approach the rich landlords who lease me houses for seven or eight months, signing the receipts on which they themselves have put stamps."

Clothes and food were another matter, yet when money was needed for these necessities of life, it always arrived at the right time and in the correct amount.

"I can see the hand of God so clearly in all this," Father Pro confessed, "that I am almost afraid that they will not kill me in all these comings and goings. This would mean a real disappointment for me because I am just longing to pop off to heaven and play *arpeggios* on my guitar with my guardian angel."

More difficult was the task of finding homes for abandoned infants. At least six of these were given to Father Pro to be put up for adoption. Unfamiliar with the ways of six-month-old infants, the priest put the first such child on the seat of the car in which he was traveling at the moment. "At the first jolt of the vehicle," he later said, "the little one went flying up into space and had I not caught it in mid-air I would probably have had to take it to the cemetery! I decided to hold it in my arms the whole time, but I have no need to tell you how wet my clothes were by the time I gave it to its new foster parents!"

The sixth child, Josè de Jesus, was so charming that the Pro family kept him with them for some time until his adoption could be arranged. Ana Maria was still caring for this child when her brothers were arrested and killed. Later a home was found for Josè.

The House of the Good Shepherd was another of Father Pro's special charities. Here girls with spiritual and emotional needs and children who had been abandoned were cared for by the sisters. Soon after his arrival in the city, the priest paid his first visit to the convent because he had learned that the nuns kept the Blessed Sacrament in their chapel at all times. There he went to pray and to beg for prayers. In return for such favors he sent food and sometimes a movie for their entertainment. He also served as a confessor for the house and once sent the following encouraging note to a young woman who was severely tempted to give up her struggle to reform: "Take courage," he advised. "Do not give way to despair. Our blessed Lady who has given you the strength to take the first steps along the road of virtue will never abandon you. We are sure to be granted what we pray for." To another he wrote, "Let yourself be conducted by Mary to the Heart of Jesus whose wound is open for you to hide yourself in. The arms of Jesus, nailed to the cross, can never be closed against you." To a dying penitent, he sent probably the most touching words of all: "You will leave this world which has made you suffer so much. The Good Shepherd opens his arms to you. Your past life, however sinful it may have been, must not worry you in the least. It has all been forgiven. You have purified it all by your bodily suffering. Lift up your eyes and contemplate heaven from which you will intercede with God for all of us who still remain down here, for all of us who have known you and who have loved you. Offer up all that you still have to suffer in this life for the welfare of your family, for the restoration of peace in our poor country and for this poor sinner."

Chapter Twelve

During the sixteen months of his ministry in Mexico City, Father Pro had to avoid arrest by the police. All Catholics who gathered in private homes to assist at Mass and receive the sacraments were in danger of being seized by police. They were charged with the task of enforcing the "Calles law" which forbade such assemblies. But the priest's ability to remain calm in the midst of danger and to hide his identity through various disguises made it possible for him to escape detection during that entire time. It was his custom, for example, to light a cigarette as soon as he stepped from a house in which he had said Mass or distributed Communion. A quick glance in all directions told him whether or not the house was being watched. If a secret agent lounged nearby, the quick-witted priest had to act quickly and decisively to allay suspicion or evade his pursuer.

"I look so much like a student," he told one of his friends, "that no one can possibly guess my real profession. Day and night, I go from one place to another, my cane in my hand and followed by a beautiful dog. I ride my brother's bicycle, which has given me a bad wound on the arm and a bump on the head." Although he prayed to be put into jail and to suffer martyrdom, Father Pro never spoke about this in his daily life but went about his work obediently and cautiously as his superiors commanded. He was well aware of the fact that if God granted him the glory of martyrdom such would be a gift in spite of all the precautions his hard-working servant had taken. He awaited martyrdom because he fervently asked for it in prayer, but he knew that if it came at last, it would be given directly from God and when God wanted it. Priests were so few that the loss of one would deprive many Christians of the sacraments. Furthermore, Father Miguel Agustin lived with his family. To endanger his life was to place the lives of Humberto and Roberto in jeopardy since their work in the League for the Defense of Religious Liberty was well known.

On December 4, 1926, Father Pro's desire to suffer for Christ was partially granted. Members of the League for the Defense of Religious Liberty released hundreds of white paper balloons that went soaring five hundred feet into the air. With spectacular explosions, they blew up releasing over the excited spectators a whole flurry of red, green and white religious pamphlets. Months had been required to plan, rehearse and carry out the operation and thousands of people had been involved in it. Two of these were Humberto and Roberto Pro. President Calles, furious at the content of the papers which criticized his government for its persecution of the Church, ordered all of the known active League members arrested. Since the Pro brothers had long been engaged in this work, their home was soon visited by the police with orders to arrest any man entering the house. "I was the only one who returned home at 11:00 a.m.," Father Pro later wrote, "so I was the only one of my family who had the honor of paying a visit to the elegant mansion of Santiago Tlaltelolco (prison). What memories! At seven o'clock that night, I was escorted away between two files of soldiers and, followed by six other individuals, arrested as I was on account of the balloon affair." This was to be the only arrest of Father Pro during his ministry in Mexico before the final imprisonment preceding his death. Since no charge was made against him, he was found not guilty. Neither was he fingerprinted or photographed on this occasion. After his release, the incident was quickly forgotten by the police.

Father Pro described his brief stay:

The officer who received us began by reading aloud the official notice of the government declaring us prisoners, then added with a sneer: "Tomorrow we will have Mass here."

"Bad luck!" I said to myself. "They had detected my profession."

"Mass?" we all asked in chorus, with the most surprised looks we could manage.

"Yes," answered the lieutenant. "There is a priest among you."

"Worse still. The matter is getting very complicated," I thought. The prisoners looked from one to the other as if to see which was the priest.

"The priest is called Miguel Agustin," the officer continued.

"Hold on there," I shouted. "I am Miguel Agustin but there is just about as much chance of my saying Mass tomorrow as there is of our sleeping on a mattress tonight!"

"Then what about this?" said the officer, pointing out the word, "Pbro."

"Oh, that is just my surname! Pro not Pbro." [Mexican clergy added Pbro to their names to signify "priest."]

Night fell. We spent the night in the open out in the courtyard because the order of arrest specified: "Make life hard for the prisoners." God knows how well this order was carried out! A huge bed of cement, that is to say, the whole courtyard was put at our disposal.

We huddled together, all seven of us, because the cold was really intense. We began by saying the rosary. Then we sang all that we knew, both hymns and songs, without in the least caring about the guards. Finally we finished by dozing a little. I remembered how impatient I used to become in Granada when I was observing the stars from the observatory and they passed by so quickly. Now, however, they seemed to be moving by in slow motion.

The following morning they intended waking us up with buckets full of cold water, but as we were not asleep you can well imagine that we jumped up at the first threat of water while the soldiers stood around laughing and hissing.

We had only three pesos and six centavos among all of us, just enough to pay for a pot of orange leaves without sugar. This, however, tasted like nectar to us at that moment. We were frozen so stiff and our skin was as tight as a drum's.

At midday I left the prison. My companions were less fortunate and did not leave until the next day. I had to appear twice to make my declaration. What did I have to declare? I never did find that out. Bandala asked me if I was ready to pay a heavy fine "Because," he said, "Señor Calles is very angry about the affair of the balloons."

"No sir," I answered, "and for two reasons. First, because I have no money and then because even if I did have the money, for no cause whatever would I carry down to the grave with me the remorse of having helped to sustain this government with even a farthing from my pocket!"

After this comedy, I had to reduce my ministries a

little. However, I managed to make some good preparation for Christmas in six homes and in the Good Shepherd with homilies, benediction and Communions.

Realizing that Father Pro had narrowly escaped with his life in the recent confrontation with police, his superiors ordered him into hiding. In a tiny room, he obediently suffered. "Why can't our ardent desires be put into practice?" he asked a young friend. "Here I am shut up in a small room with nothing to do during these long hours of waiting. It is enough to destroy all my energy! My only consolation is that of praying for those who are working for the good cause.

"Time goes by, languid and silent, like a gray cloud in the wintertime. I look out into the street: the world bustles by. I hear the grating of the trams as they roll on their way at high speed. Larks slide through the sky. So here I am with my arms crossed, looking out into empty space just like a pebble encrusted in a mountain

"I know now why the jaguar hurls itself against the railing of its cage. I know why the hyena bites the bars of its prison. I understand the despair of the boa caught in the snare. They all prefer death to inactivity.

"Those who retain me here do not realize the fire that burns within me. However it is necessary for the soul to go through the trial of solitude and repose."

When he was able to return to his active life, he was once again observed by the police. One morning at a "Eucharistic Station," he was surprised by the cry of a servant girl who rushed into the room to announce that the police were coming.

"The congregation became quite frightened," Father Pro noted, "and turned white with fright.

"Be calm," I told them. "Hide your veils. Disperse into different rooms and above all keep quiet!"

"That day, I was wearing a cap and a gray overcoat which

had become quite dirty. I took out a cigarette which I fitted into a long cigarette holder. I hid the Blessed Sacrament over my heart and awaited the intruders.

"There is public veneration going on here," the police said.

"Come along now, you are mocking me," Father Pro replied.

"There is a public service going on here!" they insisted.

"No, but it wouldn't be a bad idea," said the priest.

"We have seen a priest enter this house."

"Humbug! I'll bet you there is no priest here."

"We have orders to search the house. Follow us!"

Father Pro encouraged them to do just that and assured them that if they found public worship going on, they should inform him so that he might participate in it!

"Then," he added, "to prevent something worse, I accompanied them. I indicated what was to be found behind each closed door, but as it was my first visit to the house I was nearly always mistaken. I announced a bedroom when it was a study; then as a sewing room what proved to be a bathroom!

"Of course the priest was not to be found anywhere but the persistent police mounted a guard at the front door. I bade them farewell, saying that if it were not for the fact that my girl friend was waiting for me I would have stayed with them until they came across the insolent priest who dared to deceive such conscientious officers.

"When I returned from my round of Holy Communions, I found them still there at the door, but the famous priest had not yet turned up!"

On Holy Thursday, 1927, Father Pro had a much narrower escape. "When I finished giving the last sermon of the retreat [to government workers]," he wrote, "I went out into the street and two policemen in plain clothes followed me. I managed to escape by a real miracle. My hour had not yet come, but only God knows how this lively adventure is going to finish!

"It was the night that I was giving a retreat to civil servants. I left them at about half-past nine. I was as red as a tomato for I had shouted myself hoarse. I saw two individuals waiting for me at the corner. I said to myself: 'This time, my son, say goodbye to your skin.' However I remembered the old saying: 'Whoever makes the first move makes also the second.' I went up to them and asked for a match.

"You can buy matches over there in the shop," they answered gruffly.

"Puffing myself out more than fat old Amoz, I turned around and walked off. They followed me. I turned around to the right and they did the same.

"This time things are serious," I said to myself. "If only I had a bicycle!"

"I took a taxi. They took one too. Luckily for me, my driver was a Catholic. As soon as he realized the fix I was in, he offered to help me.

"Listen, my son," I said, "slow down at the corner I will show you. I will jump out and you will drive on. I put my cap into my pocket, unbuttoned my jacket so as to show my white shirt and then jumped. I fell over, of course, but got on my feet in a flash and leaned against a tree. A few seconds later, my two bloodhounds passed by so near to me that the mudguard of their taxi scratched me. They saw me, no doubt, but did not dream that it was I. I turned back and walked off, not as sprightly as I would have liked to, because the blow I received on falling out of the taxi was beginning to make itself felt."

One morning while he was on his way to celebrate Mass in a private home, he discovered that the front door was guarded by two policemen. To enter the house where people waited for him was to run great risk. To walk away would show fear. So Father Pro walked up to the police, pulled out a notebook and wrote down the number of the house. In the dusky half-light of dawn, he flipped the lapel of his coat indicating that there was a police badge there and said, "There is a cat in the box here."

The two men gave him a crisp military salute and let him enter the house. Bounding up the stairs, he found his huddled friends pale with fright. Instantly they surrounded him and tried to push him into a dark cupboard that he realized was full of cockroaches. The priest would not hear of such imprisonment and began to make preparations for celebrating Mass. The faithful refused to allow such a thing because of the danger.

"I tired myself telling them that we had never been so safe as then," he concluded, "with the police mounting guard at our very door. There was nothing to be done. I tucked my cassock under my arm and went out the same way I had come in. Then, with my eternal cigarette, I made a sort of spin by way of a salute. I received two superb military salutes from my policemen."

Even in private homes where he studied and heard confessions, Father Pro was never safe. The danger of an informer was constant. Yet the priest never turned away anyone who wished to see him. One evening he looked up from the book he was studying to see a huge, heavily armed man striding into his room.

"Aren't you afraid?" his visitor asked him.

"What should I be afraid of?" Father Pro asked. "I fear sin but I am not afraid of anything else. I am not even afraid of God who is so good!"

"Aren't you afraid of me?"

"Less than of anyone else. Why should I fear you?"

"I want to see you alone," the giant visitor said.

The priest closed the door and invited him to sit down.

"No, sir, I will not sit down," the man said gruffly. "What I have to say can only be said kneeling." With that he made his confession with such contrition that tears were soon flooding his cheeks. So moved was the priest by this outpouring of heart that he found himself in tears as he gave the humble man absolution.

His ability to understand and sympathize with others can be seen in a letter he once wrote to another penitent:

> You ask me if God speaks to the soul? Of course he does and his words are extremely kind. I know that from my own experience and I assure you that I did not have your good dispositions on answering his call. On the contrary, my wickedness went to the extreme of raising all sorts of obstacles. In his infinite mercy, he looked upon this dry and barren trunk of my life and saw in the future this image which he himself would make with his grace. He gave me a religious vocation and withdrew me, in spite of myself, from the corrupt world in which I lived so as to accomplish in me those beautiful words of David: "I lifted you out of the dunghill to place you among the princes of my people." You congratulate me for having obtained these graces from heaven on your behalf? You ask what I have done that God favors you in this manner? Nothing at all. They are proofs of his pure love for you.

And to his provincial he once wrote with candor:

> In spite of my good will, there is no fear of my getting proud of what I might do. God just puts me down at the door of a house. A servant awaits me there and another shows me in. Then the owners of the house make a fuss over me because they have heard me utter profound sentences such as: "Well, really, madam, I just can't understand what it is you are asking me!" With that they take me for the wisest man of the century! It is the grace of God which works these conversions and just uses me as a tool. In this way I resolve the

most difficult cases, without ever getting to know how
or when I managed to give the solution. God himself
makes up for my deficiency.

One of the last notes he wrote shows his profound humility and trust in God.

"From my prison, the 19th of November, 1927. I shall
probably never see you again in this life. It is God who disposes it thus. I accept his designs and I bless him for all of
them. I have never judged myself necessary! I am nothing but a
poor instrument in the hands of God. If he no longer wishes to
use me, it is because he wishes to take up another!"

One of his last desires was for the restoration of Mexico
to Christ the King:

> Return to the sanctuary, O Lord,
> To the empty tabernacle that awaits you.
> Hear, O good Jesus, the cry
> Of loving souls during their Calvary!
> Attend to the cry of crucified souls
> On their cross of pain and sorrow.
> For what greater grief can come our way
> Than the lack of your divine presence?
> Sweet Savior, why did you go away?
> From the depths of our sorrow and desolation
> We cry to you, O Lord.
> Will you not hear us?
> O God, you forgive those
> Who confess their faults
> And humbly repent.
> Have pity on Mexico!
> She admits her offenses
> And humbly acclaims you King!
> Those who wounded you by their sins
> Now turn to you, Lord, repentant.
> See them humbly kneeling before you
> Imploring your pardon.

> By the tears of those who suffer for you,
> Sweet Savior, return to the sanctuary!

The desire Father Pro had long felt to give his life for Christ continued to grow intensely within him. In a beautiful prayer to our Lady, he showed his thirst in a striking manner.

> Allow me to spend my life near you, O my Mother! Let me accompany you in your sorrow and loneliness. What I earnestly desire along the road of my life is not the joy of Bethlehem, nor that of adoring the Child Jesus in your virginal arms. I do not ask to enjoy the loving presence of Jesus in the humble house of Nazareth, nor to join the choirs of angels in the glory of your Assumption. What I really want in my life is the mocking and sneering of Calvary. I desire the slow agony of your Son, the contempt, the disgrace and the infamy of the cross. What I desire, O most sorrowful Virgin, is to stand close to you, so as to fortify my spirit by your tears. I want to consummate my sacrifice by your martyrdom, sustain my heart by your solitude and love my God and your God by the immolation of my whole being.

That prayer was written November 13, 1927. Before the sun set behind the blue rim of mountains that surround beautiful Mexico City, his prayer was to be heard. In the loud explosion of a bomb and the sharp rattle of gunfire about which he knew nothing and in which he played no part, his destiny was sealed. His prayer was answered.

During the summer of 1927, General Alvaro Obregón had been elected to succeed President Calles as head of the government of Mexico. It was not the general's first term as leader of his nation. From 1920 until 1924, he had served as president, and during that period numerous attacks had been made against the Church. Bombs exploded with exasperating regularity inside churches and the homes of bishops and priests. Not even the high altar of the Basilica of Our Lady of Guadalupe escaped attack. After each incident, little effort was made to discover or punish the culprits. News that this same man would soon return to rule caused consternation among Catholics, and one young engineer decided to do something drastic to prevent it.

With three companions, Luis Segura Vilchis drove a small Essex past the sleek Cadillac of General Obregón on Sunday afternoon, November 13th, and tossed two homemade bombs against his car. A whole round of revolver ammunition clattered against the president-elect's vehicle also. Yet, miraculously, neither he or his bodyguards were killed. Emerging from the smoke and ruins of the demolished automobile, Obregón found that he suffered from only minor cuts and bruises. A second car of bodyguards sped forward in pursuit of the Essex. In the gun battle that followed, one of the attackers, Nahum Ruiz, was shot in the head. He collapsed unconscious, bleeding profusely over Juan Tirado. Overtaken by their pursuers, the conspirators crashed their car into another and fled. The driver of the Essex vanished into the confused crowd that quickly formed. He was never to be found. Segura Vilchis shook off his pursuers and went to a bullfight. Nahum Ruiz was carried under guard to a hospital, and bloodstained Juan Tirado soon found himself in the police station being questioned and later frightfully tortured.

Not until evening did Father Pro or his brothers hear of the attack. Humberto and Roberto had spent the day in the country while Father Pro went about his duties of hearing confessions and visiting friends. It was a newspaper report that brought them the ominous news that the car used in the attack was an Essex with license plate 10101. Until only a few days before, Humberto had owned this car and used it for his work in the League for the Defense of Religious Liberty. He had sold it to Luis Segura Vilchis, but he realized now that the police would soon be checking its former owners. Although the Essex had been registered under an assumed name, he was certain that they would have ways and means of discovering his previous ownership.

As the search continued for any members of the League who might have played a part in the assassination attempt, the Pros left their house on Panuco Street and separated to find lodging with different families. With a small note stating: "Do not go to Panuco," Father Pro canceled a Holy Hour and slipped quietly into hiding with his brothers. On Tuesday, the police apprehended Segura Vilchis who gave the following testimony:

> It is I who prepared and made the bombs that were thrown at Obregón. I, too, chose my companions. Two of them are already in the hands of the police and the third has taken flight. I myself bought the material used in the making of the bombs. The three men who went with me in the car are the only people who knew anything about my project. There had been no previous meetings to decide on the plan. I declare that I assume all the moral and material responsibility for the assault and that I was the only inventor and organizer.

Not one word was said of the Pro brothers nor would later testimony mention them. The reason for this is that they had nothing to do with the plot. Although they worked in the same League as Vilchis, they never approved of military means to accomplish their purposes. In the home of Señora Maria Valdes, Father Pro found a more secure hiding place for his brothers, and there he said his last three Masses. There also he heard confessions of a few who came seeking him, but this troubled Señora Valdes who feared that someone would betray him, as later happened. As the days dragged by, the three men made their plans. Roberto and Humberto were to attempt exile in the United States while Father Pro would return to his apostolate in disguise. The plans were to come to nothing.

Before dawn of November 18, the house of Maria Valdes was surrounded by heavily armed police. Soon they were inside, and the butts of their rifles were banging against the door of the room shared by Father Pro and his brothers. Awakened so rudely from sleep, the priest's first thought was to help Roberto and Humberto. "Be sorry for your sins," he told them. "I am going to give you absolution." He pronounced the formula and made the sign of the cross. "Let us offer up our lives to God for religious liberty in Mexico," he told them. "Let us make our offering together and may God deign to accept it."

When one of the officers accused Señora Valdes of harboring conspirators, she denied it stating, "What I do know is that I was hiding a holy priest." Father Pro came at once to her defense, saying, "This woman has done nothing at all. Let her go in peace and do as you please with us." With that he went to the cupboard that contained his priestly vestments. He took out a small crucifix, kissed it and slipped it into his pocket. "They are going to shoot me," he told Señora Valdes quietly. "I confide to you my priestly vestments."

When told to put on his cloak, the priest assured his captors that he was not cold, but he did take the serape which Señora Valdes offered him. Once in prison he gave it to the tormented Tirado who wore it finally to his death.

Having blessed Señora Valdes and her maids, Father Pro said loudly as he moved out into the darkness with his brothers, "Blessed be God! Blessed be the Virgin of Guadalupe."

They soon found themselves locked securely in basement cells of the police station. Sharing cell No. 1 with Roberto and later with others, Father Pro could not have been favorably impressed by his new surroundings "It was a damp, cold hole," a fellow prisoner later testified, "five feet wide by ten feet long. The sun never entered there. A horrible smell reached it from the lavatories. There was poor ventilation and darkness."

Having heard of her brothers' arrest, Ana Maria brought food to them each day, but this reached them cold and cut into small pieces as the guards searched without success for hidden messages within it. Only once did Ana Maria see Father Miguel Agustin during his five days of imprisonment. One day he was being led to the offices for yet another interrogation. As he made his way up the stairs, he caught sight of her and waved to her. It was their last meeting.

"I had never met Father Pro before," Antonio Mutiozabal, a fellow prisoner, remarked. "I often saw him praying in his dungeon. At night, he made us all pray. We also sang the *March of Saint Ignatius.* He told me and his brothers that we must forgive our enemies. Father Pro was resigned, patient and even happy. He told us that we should be happy to suffer something for the love of Jesus Christ, and if we had even more to suffer, if we were shot, for example, that we should be proud of dying for Christ. As for himself, he was longing for that wonderful lot to fall his way. He spent his last night stretched out on the floor. He had given me his straw mattress."

That same night there was much activity in the prison. The windows of the cells were boarded up so that the prisoners could not see the preparations being made for their deaths. No court trial had taken place; no sentence had been passed. Reporters and photographers from the newspaper, *Excelsior*, arrived and Father Pro spoke briefly with them.

"Are you a priest?" he was asked by a reporter.

"Yes, sir. A Jesuit priest."

"Have you anything to declare?"

"No, nothing. I am grateful for the attention I have received from those who arrested me. I have had nothing to do with this affair of the assault, because I am a lover of order. I am quite at peace, and I am sure that justice will be done sooner or later. I deny having taken any part whatever in this plot." Photographs were taken for the morning edition, and then the visitors were ushered out of the dark, forbidding prison.

November 23th dawned hazy and cold. Father Pro awoke with a throbbing headache after his night on the cold, bare floor. "I feel something is going to happen today," he told Roberto. "Let us ask God for the necessary grace." At 9:30 a.m. the soldiers of the firing squad arrived along with members of General Cruz's staff, who were to see that the execution was carried out according to the president Calles' orders. Photographers and reporters rushed around and persons invited to view the execution began to arrive. At 10:20, Father Pro heard his name called. He shook hands with Roberto and followed his guards out of the prison into the sun-drenched patio. His dark eyes swept in everything at once: the rough log fence at the far end of the yard with its crude steel targets before which he would stand, the soldiers with their rifles, the hushed crowd and the photographers with their cumbersome cameras. He was dressed in a tattered brown suit, a tan sweater and a blue tie, and was badly in need of a shave after five days in prison. Miguel Agustin made his way to the wall facing the firing squad. Asked if he had a final wish, he said simply, "Yes, I would like to pray for a while." He sank to his knees, made a slow sign of the cross and prayed fervently with bowed head and crossed arms. He kissed his crucifix. Then he was ready.

He stood up with his crucifix in one hand, a rosary in the other, turned to face the rifles and refused to be blindfolded. Slowly he raised his arms out at his sides until his body took the form of a cross. His lips moved in prayer, and he indicated that he was ready.

"Aim!" shouted the officer. "Fire!"

The rifles hurled five bullets that tore through his heart. His arms fell slowly, and he sank quietly backward to the ground like a tired child into his father's arms. A doctor appeared at once and ordered the *coup de grace* which a soldier gave with a rifle at point-blank range.

In quick succession Segura Vilchis, Humberto Pro and Juan Tirado were led forward to sudden death. Even to this day no one knows why Roberto's life was spared. He remained in prison for a time and later was ordered into temporary exile.

Forbidden entrance to the prison but able to hear the shots, Ana Maria waited helplessly for news of the events inside. In the restless crowd a lawyer stood holding a stay of execution for the prisoners. His pleas for admittance went unheeded. The document that could have saved the lives of the Pro brothers proved worthless.

That afternoon, the bodies of Father Miguel Agustin and Humberto Pro were returned to their father's house on Panuco Street. An endless stream of visitors filed past them with prayers and flowers and wreaths during most of the night. Priests came out of hiding to lead the prayers for burial the following afternoon, and the funeral cortege became a march of triumph for the martyred dead. "There was nothing mournful about the ceremony," stated an eyewitness. "Cheering could be heard on all sides. People came out onto the balconies and threw flowers in the street as the coffins passed by. All the way along, people could be seen kneeling down at the street corners. It was really like a Corpus Christi procession."

Thousands of people filled the streets to watch the procession pass. Thousands more waited in the cemetery. In the crypt reserved for the Jesuit dead, Father Pro's body was laid to rest. Nearby, in a small plot of land reserved for the Pro family, the body of Humberto was prayerfully buried. "It is over," venerable old Señor Pro said at last. "Let us give praise to God!"

In the years that followed, a constant stream of visitors came to the tomb of Father Miguel Agustin Pro—the sick, the poor, the workers. So many favors were attributed to his prayers to God, that an ecclesiastical examination of his cause was begun in 1934. Completed two years later, the documents and conclusions were accepted favorably by Rome. In 1952, Pope Pius XII signed the decree of introduction of the cause. Since that time, an even more painstaking examination has been made into the life, work and virtues of Father Pro. The work for his cause still continues and may soon be brought to glorious fruition. Meanwhile, his fame continues to spread throughout the world. His love for the poor, the workers, the young, the sick, the tempted and the spiritually weak attract many hearts to him. His good sense, wit, zeal and humor make him a model for the youth of today who, like him, have such high ideals and will not be content until they have tried to attain them with sincerity, generosity and joy.

 **auline** *BOOKS & MEDIA*

ALASKA
750 West 5th Ave., Anchorage, AK 99501; 907-272-8183

CALIFORNIA
3908 Sepulveda Blvd., Culver City, CA 90230; 310-397-8676
5945 Balboa Ave., San Diego, CA 92111; 619-565-9181
46 Geary Street, San Francisco, CA 94108; 415-781-5180

FLORIDA
145 S.W. 107th Ave., Miami, FL 33174; 305-559-6715

HAWAII
1143 Bishop Street, Honolulu, HI 96813; 808-521-2731

ILLINOIS
172 North Michigan Ave., Chicago, IL 60601; 312-346-4228

LOUISIANA
4403 Veterans Memorial Blvd., Metairie, LA 70006; 504-887-7631

MASSACHUSETTS
50 St. Paul's Ave., Jamaica Plain, Boston, MA 02130; 617-522-8911
Rte. 1, 885 Providence Hwy., Dedham, MA 02026; 617-326-5385

MISSOURI
9804 Watson Rd., St. Louis, MO 63126; 314-965-3512

NEW JERSEY
561 U.S. Route 1, Wick Plaza, Edison, NJ 08817; 908-572-1200

NEW YORK
150 East 52nd Street, New York, NY 10022; 212-754-1110
78 Fort Place, Staten Island, NY 10301; 718-447-5071

OHIO
2105 Ontario Street, Cleveland, OH 44115; 216-621-9427

PENNSYLVANIA
Northeast Shopping Center, 9171-A Roosevelt Blvd., Philadelphia, PA
19114; 215-676-9494

SOUTH CAROLINA
243 King Street, Charleston, SC 29401; 803-577-0175

TENNESSEE
4811 Poplar Ave., Memphis, TN 38117; 901-761-2987

TEXAS
114 Main Plaza, San Antonio, TX 78205; 210-224-8101

VIRGINIA
1025 King Street, Alexandria, VA 22314; 703-549-3806

CANADA
3022 Dufferin Street, Toronto, Ontario, Canada M6B 3T5; 416-781-9131